THE UNITED STATES

LAKE SUPERIOR

Mississippi River

LAKE HURON

LAKE MICHIGAN

Wisconsin River

Des Moines River

Illinois River

Missouri River

OZARK PLATEAU

Mississippi River

Tennessee River

Wabash River

Ohio River

LAKE ONTARIO

LAKE ERIE

ALLEGHENY MOUNTAINS

Hudson River

CAPE COD

Delaware River

LONG ISLAND

Potomac River

CHESAPEAKE BAY

APPALACHIAN MOUNTAINS

CAPE HATTERAS

Savannah River

PIEDMONT PLATEAU

Chattahoochee River

ATLANTIC OCEAN

Mississippi River

GULF OF MEXICO

Lake Okeechobee

FLORIDA KEYS

THE UNITED STATES

By the Editors of Time-Life Books
With photographs by Winnie Denker

TIME-LIFE BOOKS · AMSTERDAM

TIME-LIFE BOOKS INC.

EDITOR: George Constable
Executive Editor: George Daniels
Director of Design: Louis Klein
Editorial Board: Roberta R. Conlan, Ellen Phillips,
Gerry Schremp, Gerald Simons, Rosalind Stubenberg,
Kit van Tulleken, Henry Woodhead
Editorial General Manager: Neal Goff
Director of Research: Phyllis K. Wise
Director of Photography: John Conrad Weiser

PRESIDENT: Reginald K. Brack Jr.
Senior Vice President: William Henry
Vice Presidents: George Artandi, Stephen L. Bair,
Robert A. Ellis, Juanita T. James, Christopher T.
Linen, James L. Mercer, Joanne A. Pello,
Paul R. Stewart

LIBRARY OF NATIONS

EDITOR: Dale M. Brown
Designers: Thomas S. Huestis, Raymond Ripper
Chief Researcher: Jane Edwin

Editorial Staff for *The United States*
Associate Editors: Jim Hicks, David S. Thomson (text);
Jane Speicher Jordan (pictures)
Staff Writer: Roberta R. Conlan
Researchers: Elise Ritter-Gibson (principal), Karin
Kinney, Denise Li, Rita Mullin, Paula York-Soderlund
Assistant Designer: Robert K. Herndon
Copy Coordinator: Margery duMond
Picture Coordinator: Linda Lee
Editorial Assistant: Myrna E. Traylor

Special Contributors: The chapter texts were written by
Ezra Bowen, Ron Bailey, Donald Dale Jackson, Richard
Stengel, Bryce Walker and Bernard Weisberger. *Other
Contributors:* LaVerle Berry, Rosemary George, Philip
Payne and A. B. C. Whipple.

Editorial Operations
Design: Ellen Robling (assistant director)
Copy Room: Diane Ullius
Production: Anne B. Landry (director), Celia Beattie
Quality Control: James J. Cox (director), Sally Collins
Library: Louise D. Forstall

Correspondents: Elisabeth Kraemer-Singh (Bonn);
Margot Hapgood, Dorothy Bacon (London); Miriam
Hsia (New York); Maria Vincenza Aloisi, Josephine du
Brusle (Paris); Ann Natanson (Rome).

CONSULTANTS

Russel B. Nye, Distinguished Professor
Emeritus at Michigan State University, is the
author of dozens of books and articles about
United States history and culture, including a
Pulitzer Prize-winning biography of 19th
Century historian George Bancroft.

William A. Cox is the Congressional Research
Service's Senior Specialist for Economic Policy.
A former Deputy Chief Economist of the U.S.
Department of Commerce, he has written
numerous articles on the American economy.

PHOTOGRAPHER: Danish-born
photographer Winnie Denker has traveled the
world for more than 10 years, taking pictures
for such diverse publications as *Paris-Match,
Marie-Claire* and *Parents* magazines. She has
worked in Bali, Samoa, India, Egypt and
Kashmir. She spent more than two months
touring the United States for this volume in the
Library of Nations series.

First printing.

Printed in U.S.A.
Published simultaneously in Canada.
School and library distribution by Silver Burdett
Company, Morristown, New Jersey.

TIME-LIFE is a trademark of Time Incorporated U.S.A.

ISBN 0-8094-5303-7 (lib. bdg.)

COVER: Silhouetted against a wide, still-glowing Western sky, a Kansas farmer stops his pick-up truck at dusk to collect the day's mail from his roadside mailbox.

PAGES 1 AND 2: On page 1 is the United States' official emblem, or Great Seal, which in addition to the national bird, a bald eagle, includes the country's motto, *"E pluribus unum"* — "Out of the many, one." The national flag is shown on page 2.

FRONT AND BACK ENDPAPERS: A topographic map showing the major rivers, plains, mountain ranges and other natural features of the United States appears on the front endpaper; the back endpaper shows the states and other political divisions.

This volume is one in a series of books describing countries of the world, their lands, peoples, histories, economies and governments.

CONTENTS

Introduction   16

PICTURE ESSAYS

1 Land of New Beginnings
19

Love Affair with the Open Road   42

2 Seeking a More Perfect Union
55

3 An Economy of Abundance
71

Harvest of Good Living   84

4 Arts with Mass Appeal
93

Sound of a City's Soul   107

5 The Power Structure
115

Redefining Women's Roles   126

6 The American Dream
137

A Diversity of Religions   150

Acknowledgments   156
Picture Credits   156
Bibliography   156
Index   158

Rimmed by docks and bridges, New York's Manhattan Island glimmers in the early-morning light. The round fort at its southern tip *(bottom, centre*

left) served as a processing centre for immigrants entering the United States from Europe before facilities on nearby Ellis Island were built.

A BURGEONING OF SERVICES

As early as 1950, the productivity of U.S. farms and factories allowed more than 50 per cent of the work force to labour in service industries—a category including everything from medical care to fast-food operations. Three decades later 67 per cent of all workers were in services, while increased mechanization cut the number of farm workers to scarcely 3.6 per cent of the total and industrial workers to 29.3 per cent.

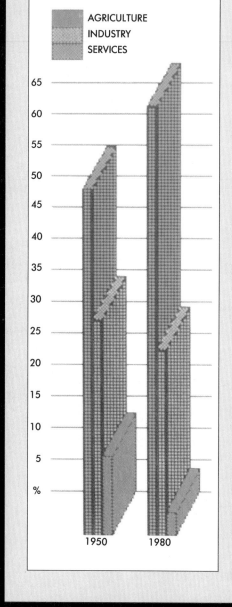

AGRICULTURE
INDUSTRY
SERVICES

65
60
55
50
45
40
35
30
25
20
15
10
5
%

1950   1980

A specialized part of the huge U.S. service industry, a 7-Eleven grocery purveys snacks, staples and other goods to customers in Dallas, Texas. Once

open from 7 a.m. to 11 p.m.—thus the name—most of the 7,000 stores in the 7-Eleven chain now serve the public 24 hours a day.

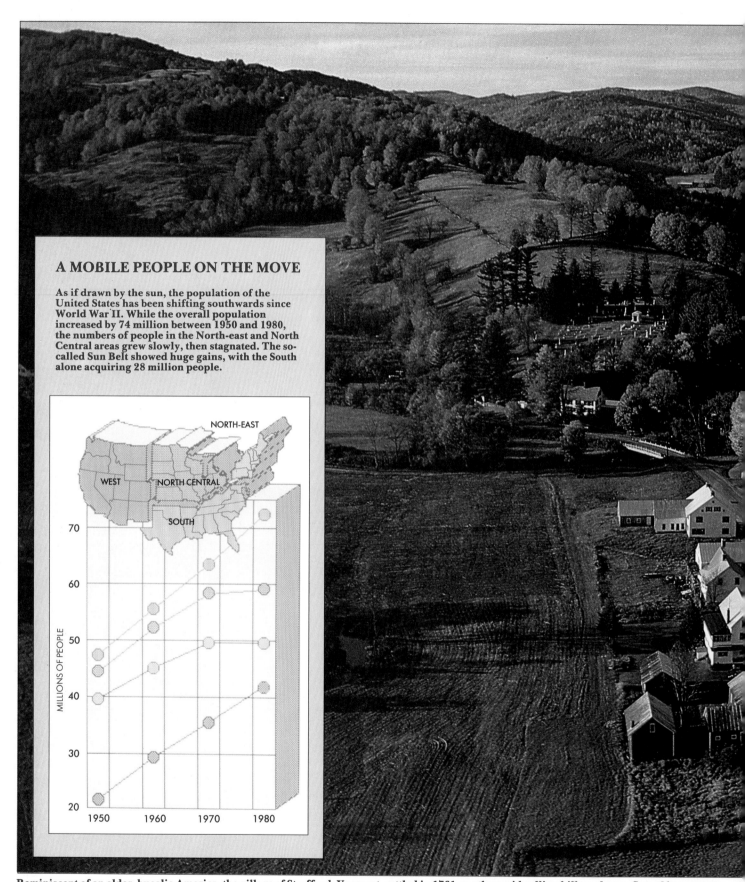

A MOBILE PEOPLE ON THE MOVE

As if drawn by the sun, the population of the
United States has been shifting southwards since
World War II. While the overall population
increased by 74 million between 1950 and 1980,
the numbers of people in the North-east and North
Central areas grew slowly, then stagnated. The so-
called Sun Belt showed huge gains, with the South
alone acquiring 28 million people.

NORTH-EAST

WEST   NORTH CENTRAL

SOUTH

MILLIONS OF PEOPLE

70

60

50

40

30

20

1950   1960   1970   1980

Reminiscent of an older, bucolic America, the village of Strafford, Vermont, settled in 1761, nestles amid rolling hills and trees flamed by autumn.

Vermont remains the least urban of all 50 states; 66.2 per cent of its people live as their ancestors did, on farms and in small towns.

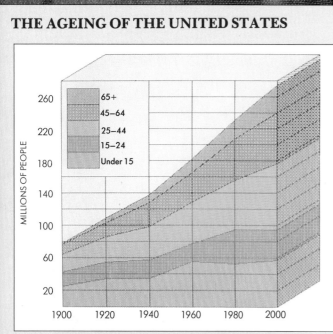

THE AGEING OF THE UNITED STATES

Largely because of improved diet and medical care, the proportion of U.S. citizens in the upper age bracket has risen over the past few decades, as the chart shows. By 1950, people 65 and older made up 4 per cent of the population; by the early 1980s, they were 11 per cent.

Two elderly sisters, both of whom are more than 100 years old, stand together on the porch of their house in the hamlet of Two Egg, Florida.

13

A section of the 1,290-kilometre-long trans-Alaskan pipeline snakes through a pass in the Brooks Range, not far from its beginning in the oilfields

PRODIGAL PRODUCTION OF ENERGY

Consuming more energy than any other nation, the U.S. leads its global competitors in energy production—with the notable exception of oil. It mines marginally more coal than the two other leading coal producers, the U.S.S.R. and China, and has tapped more natural gas than anyone else. And it produces vastly more kilowatts of electricity than even its nearest rival, the U.S.S.R. But both Russia and Saudi Arabia pump more oil than the U.S., despite new sources in Alaska's Arctic.

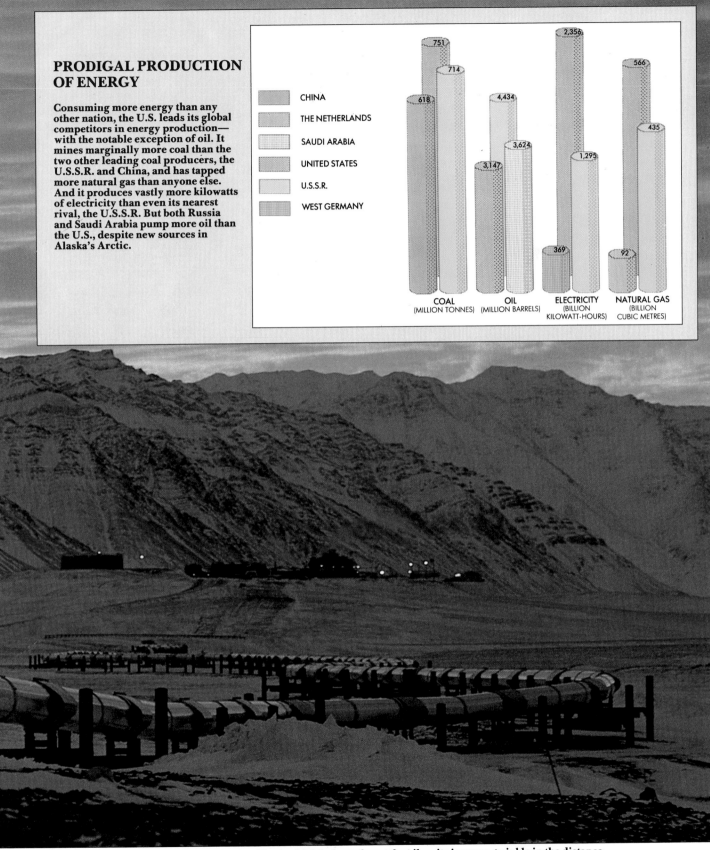

CHINA

THE NETHERLANDS

SAUDI ARABIA

UNITED STATES

U.S.S.R.

WEST GERMANY

COAL (MILLION TONNES)

OIL (MILLION BARRELS)

ELECTRICITY (BILLION KILOWATT-HOURS)

NATURAL GAS (BILLION CUBIC METRES)

around Prudhoe Bay. The lights of Pump Station No. 4, which helps to boost the oil on its journey, twinkle in the distance.

15

"Give me your tired, your poor,/Your huddled masses yearning to breathe free," run the lines on the base of the Statue of Liberty. Though written a century ago, they are as meaningful today as then. Indeed, they contain one of the core truths about the United States: that it is a nation built by people who came from somewhere else, almost all with the same purpose—to better themselves.

The freedom the immigrants sought and found was not just political and religious; it was social. They were released from the class restraints of the Old World. A poor English weaver, who had emigrated in 1830 to New York State, wrote in a letter home to his wife: "America is not like England, for here no man thinks himself your superior. An American, however low his station, never feels himself abashed when entering the presence of the highest. This is a country where a man can stand as a man, and where he can enjoy the fruits of his own exertions, with rational liberty to the fullest extent." (A glaring exception to this cheerful situation was America's population of black slaves; but in time, their fight for freedom and liberty would reconfirm the nation's ideals.)

Continually revitalized by fresh infusions of immigrants, America could draw on the rich personal resources of all the newcomers to challenge a succession of frontiers. First there was the *frontier*, the one that demarcated the extent of pioneer settlement of the American wilderness. Land-seeking European immigrants pouring in through Atlantic ports pushed this frontier further and further west—and its movement was greatly accelerated by the work of other immigrants, from China, who helped to build the railways that carried many settlers to the new territory.

In little more than a century, the population of the U.S. increased by almost 20 times, from 3.9 million in 1790 to 75.9 million in 1900. This frontier era was marked by violence; the settlers almost exterminated the Indians, grabbing their land and destroying their cultures and means of existence. But it was also a time of courage and promise that gave rise to the enduring Old West ideals and myths—perhaps most notably that of the lone hero who secures justice with a fast gun—that thereafter pervaded both the foreigner's view of America and America's idea of itself.

In 1890, the U.S. Bureau of the Census formally declared that the frontier had ceased to exist. The West was not literally filled up with settlers, of course, but there was no longer a recognizable line west of which lived less than 1 person per square kilometre—the Census Bureau's definition of the frontier. Yet the inflow of people did not abate; in fact, it increased. In six of the years between 1905 and 1914, immigration exceeded a million people annually, the highest yearly totals ever. Most came from Southern and Eastern European coun-

16

tries, and they helped to populate a new American frontier of expanding cities and burgeoning industries.

In the 1920s, Congress severely limited the number of foreigners who could move to the U.S. But in the reduced stream of immigrants were a significant number of intellectuals fleeing the spread of Fascism and anti-Semitism in Europe. These newcomers played crucial roles in the American exploration of yet another frontier, that of science. Among them was the German-born theoretical physicist Albert Einstein, one of the greatest scientific minds in history. They also included Enrico Fermi from Italy, who created the first nuclear chain reaction, and Hungarian-born Edward Teller, who was instrumental in the development of the hydrogen bomb.

Beginning in the late 1950s, the United States turned a substantial portion of its national energies—and wealth—to the exploration of perhaps the most exciting frontier of all: space. The space programme, which involved danger (three astronauts were killed in 1967), intense competition (national honour was at stake in a race with the Soviet Union) and a dream (putting men on the moon, fulfilled in 1969), became the new archetypal American adventure. But in space, too, the tradition of the immigrant's role in American achievement held true: one of the people who helped to make space travel possible was Wernher von Braun, a German rocket engineer who became a U.S. citizen in 1955.

Papers in hand, a mother waits anxiously with her daughter on Ellis Island in the early part of the 20th century. The immigration processing centre, located in New York Harbour, was in operation from 1892 until 1943, when World War II stemmed the flow of aliens from abroad.

As the frontier of space expands, still other frontiers are evolving. The latest is high technology, and it is outmoding many of the old, heavy "smokestack" industries and hurting cities in which they once flourished. What will be the fate of the workers who are now losing jobs to automation? And what of the cities? Can they be revived? The answers may not be clear for decades. In the meantime, the country has opened its gates to another wave of immigrants, mostly from South-East Asia and Latin America. Perhaps they can solve some of today's problems. If so, these new Americans will be reconfirming the nation's faith that each successive immigrant group is as one American has so eloquently put it, "the bearer of some mental or spiritual gift which is unique, and which we cannot afford to lose".

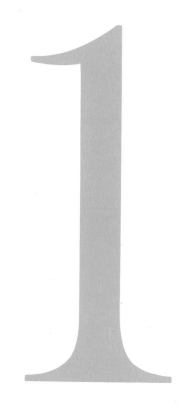

Seattle's huge domed stadium, the
Kingdome, seating 75,000 baseball
or football fans, echoes the shape of
Washington State's more famous
landmark, Mount Rainier. The
highest peak in the Cascade Range
at 4,392 metres, it looms over Seattle
although it is 160 kilometres away.

LAND OF NEW BEGINNINGS

In a cinema in East Africa not long ago, a scene in a Hollywood film prompted a woman to remark caustically, "That's America for you." The screen, as she spoke, was ablaze with the neon glare of Las Vegas, Nevada, one of America's Western gambling meccas. The woman's comment suggested to her listeners that the whole of the U.S. was like this—a gaudy concoction of tasteless commercialism.

Moments later the film contradicted her when the scene shifted to the austere expanse of adjacent desert, then upwards nearly 4,000 metres to the peaks of nearby mountains, whose snow formed a silver-white mantle to outdazzle the brightest boom-town neon. At this, a British journalist who was sitting behind the woman said: "In one sweep of the eye we've seen the likes of the Serengeti Plains and the Alps as well. It's a wonder that any American ever bothers to go abroad."

A wonder, indeed. For America embraces such a varied richness of terrain, such a range of environment, such an extraordinary breadth both of physical resource and of vista that it has been a kind of promised land from the very beginning. About 230 million people now live in the United States, and all of them or their ancestors—including the Asian forebears of the American Indians themselves—came to America from somewhere else.

To a newcomer, perhaps the most striking feature of the country is its size: 9.3 million square kilometres, making the United States the world's fourth largest nation (after the Soviet Union, Canada and China). The distance between Boston and San Francisco is greater than the distance between Paris and Baghdad.

America's vastness has been crucial both in luring people from abroad and in shaping American attitudes and aspirations. From the top of a tractor on the table-flat Great Plains, nothing stops the eye through the full, 360-degree sweep of the compass; the world seems to consist of sky and sun and wheat and wind. With few, if any, limits upon one's outer vision, it is unnatural for the inner eye to perceive many limits on what a person can say or do, or how he or she may choose to live or worship.

Americans built their country in this spirit: the First Amendment of the Constitution says, with a clarity that two centuries have not much muddied: "Congress shall make no law respecting an establishment of religion, or prohibiting the free exercise thereof; or abridging the freedom of speech." From atop such principles, a human being can see forever.

Today, after some 200 years of urbanization, the sense and reality of space still exist all over the United States. Towns and cities holding more than three fourths of the entire country's population take up only 2 per cent of the land in the 48 contiguous states.

1

The author Gertrude Stein summed up this enduring elbow room succinctly: "In the United States," she wrote, "there is more land where nobody is than where anybody is."

But the strength and wonder of the U.S. lie in the land's diversity rather than its extent. Inland from the Atlantic Ocean rises a lush country of forests and mountains and grassy plains, drained by a lacework of rivers—including the Mississippi-Missouri-Ohio river system, the longest in the world—and crowned by the five connected Great Lakes. In the West, crags with glaciered flanks climb to nearly 4,500 metres, and Alaska's Mount McKinley tops 6,000 metres, higher than the highest of the Alps. Within 160 kilometres of California's Mount Whitney—at 4,418 metres the highest point in the contiguous 48 states—the

ground drops to 86 metres below sea level in the small, roasting desert known as Death Valley.

Yet extremes of geography and climate are by no means the dominant features of American life. America's diversity, although striking, is manageable. Most of the country lies in the temperate zone. There are no sweltering jungles; the nearest equivalents are patches of mangrove swamp in Florida and Louisiana. The Soviet Union and Canada have enormous reaches of arctic tundra that are all but uninhabitable, but more than four fifths of the U.S. is usable, even comfortable, space. It is a natural place for things to grow and to flourish.

And flourish they do. Noah could still collect a tremendous variety of wild beasts from the land and its adjacent waters: grizzly bears and whales,

alligators and giant California condors, grey wolves and antelope. And there is a similarly rich endowment of wild plants, including both the biggest and the oldest living things on earth: the Pacific Coast's sequoia trees, some of which tower more than 115 metres and measure 9 metres in circumference, and bristlecone pines that sprouted nearly 5,000 years ago.

In the great Mississippi-Missouri-Ohio drainage basin, the soil is so rich and dark that the poet Robert Frost described it as "good enough to eat". Good enough, at any rate, that the three states of Kansas, Nebraska and Minnesota alone produce enough meat and grain to provide a meal a day for every person in the United States and Canada throughout the year—with some left over for Mexico.

"Land is given," wrote educationist

Theodore M. Hesburgh. "It may be well or badly used. It is only the spirit and character of a people that eventually shape a land, forge a nation upon it." Americans have shaped some of their land with a vengeance—and with mixed results.

American Indians had a reverent attitude towards the land, considering it fundamentally unpossessable, but the people who arrived from other shores had no such compunctions.

They regarded the land as something for them to master. To tap the riches that lay beneath its surface, they sank shafts deep in the earth to bring up the minerals, or they simply stripped off the surface—despoiling the vegetation in the process—to get at the veins of coal lying just beneath.

More admirably, the newcomers have managed to transform uninhabitable deserts into lush garden spots. California's huge Imperial Valley once was a desiccated place that people crossed as quickly as possible. But since 1940, when the All-American Canal—part of the federal irrigation system that also includes the Hoover Dam—was completed, water has gushed into the dry soil of the valley, producing an abundance of lettuce, carrots, melons and tomatoes.

The urge to tame and fill the country's spaces has occasionally operated with astonishing speed. Could any other people, to choose one perfectly American example, have organized the Oklahoma land rush? On a wonderfully absurd morning in 1893, the U.S. government opened to settlement the last official tract of Indian Territory, 25,900 square kilometres of good grazing land known as the Cherokee Outlet. At noon on September 16, 100,000 land-hungry pioneers lined up at the Outlet's edge aboard wagons, on horses, afoot and even on bicycles, all of them intent on staking out a share of the land. A gun went off, and away they went in a cloud of dust. It was the essence of opportunism, a great game open to all, with the prime land going to the swiftest.

The diversity of all those who came to America has at times proved less manageable than the diversity of the land itself. The African slaves and their descendants have had to struggle for centuries to achieve even their present imperfect equality with white Americans—many of whose ancestors arrived long after the blacks did. Gang fights between different ethnic and racial groups have been a recurring feature in some American cities. Still, immigrants generally have been assimilated within a generation or two, as each new group got a foothold on the ladder to economic success.

Television, radio, newspapers and magazines have helped in this process of integration by instilling a common value system. The United States contains some 142 million television sets. There are two radios for every human being in the nation. Each morning some 1,700 daily papers hit the streets; the total circulation of all periodicals tops 210 million.

Another great tie binding the country together is transportation. Americans own about 106 million cars, which travel 1.77 trillion passenger kilometres each year. Moreover, they fly 362 billion annual airline passenger kilometres. Today's Americans—those who can afford to, at any rate—can travel anywhere they desire, learning about the various regions of their country as they go.

Critics contend that such mobility and the pervasive influence of radio and television, while helping to unify the United States, have also tended to homogenize the country's culture. It is certainly true that chain business establishments—McDonald's hamburgers, Holiday Inn motels, Kentucky Fried Chicken—have helped to standardize eating habits and travellers' accommodation. Thousands of near-identical shopping precincts—commercial villages with all amenities at hand—dot the suburbs. And the sounds of Muzak—the trade name for piped-in music tailored to stimulate people to buy more or to work more efficiently—are heard across the land.

As New Brunswick in New Jersey, Omaha in Nebraska, and Chula Vista in California, take to such standardization, the country's old multiplicity of local cuisines and lifestyles, as well as attitudes and even regional accents, may be vanishing. "The divisions of America—North, South, East, West—have long been blurred," wrote author Lillian Hellman. "We have moved too much, intermarried with too many other split levels, cars and freezers to leave behind anything more than pockets of the past."

Perhaps so. But if a traveller from abroad were to tour the U.S., stopping to watch and listen and think, he or she would find some surprises in the size, the spirit and the significance of these pockets. The traveller might conclude that America is not so much growing bland as simply growing up, at a cost of some youthful charm but with many of its personal and regional distinctions still intact.

The tour might begin in New England—the six states of Maine, New Hampshire, Vermont, Massachusetts, Connecticut and Rhode Island. All

Deeply furrowed bark indicates the great age—up to 3,000 years—of California's giant sequoias. About 5,000 of these huge trees, the world's largest, stand safe from the logger's axe in the 156,558-hectare Sequoia National Park, in the Sierra Nevada.

1

Scores of pleasure craft crowd the
protected harbour of Marblehead,
Massachusetts, one of New England's
oldest fishing ports. Founded in 1633,
it is now a choice suburb of Boston,
whose skyline appears on the horizon.

except landlocked Vermont share a portion of the crinkled Atlantic coastline, where cosy harbours still shelter New England's commercial fishing fleet. Today, many New Englanders sail simply for fun: on a summer weekend, thousands of pleasure crafts speckle the waters of Long Island Sound, Vineyard Sound and Buzzards Bay. But their seagoing ancestors, fishing for cod off their home shores or pursuing whales around the globe, brought the region its first prosperity.

Away from the sea, the wooded mountains cradle, here and there, a white-spired church or a patchwork of fields where cows still crop the grass right up to the stone walls. The strongest vestiges of traditional Yankee character survive in northern New England—an area that has long been inhabited by close-mouthed country people, crafty in a deal, hard-working, thrifty, conservative about family and religion but sometimes radical in politics, proud, dry-witted and hard to push around.

Perhaps the best-known exemplar of New England taciturnity was the 30th President of the United States, Calvin Coolidge, or ":Silent Cal". Anecdotes about the man are worn as smooth as river rocks. On one occasion he was presented with a garden rake by an orator who said that the implement was made of hickory wood. The orator then long-windedly compared the resiliency of hickory to the character of the new President from Vermont. Coolidge studied the rake for a long time and said, "Ash". On a train trip with the President, a companion, made restless by Coolidge's habitual silence, pointed out the window at a field full of sheep and noted, "The sheep have been sheared." Coolidge's cool reply was:

"Looks like it from this side."

The true Yankee is the honest heir to the values of New England's founding Puritans, with their high regard for work, church, community and righteousness. Today many of those values still survive, although the New Englanders have changed, as has much of their countryside. It is hard to find an outward trace of the old Yankee in some parts of the highly urbanized southern New England state of Connecticut, at least in the heavily Italian industrial crush of New Haven or among the clerks of giant insurance companies in Hartford. Many of the strong-handed families who farm in the Connecticut Valley, New England's major agricultural area, have ways analogous to those of the Yankee, but their roots are still in Poland.

Not even Boston, queen city of New England, retains much that is purely Yankee, except for a patrician cadre referred to as the Brahmins. These are the long-established moneyed families who once ran the city and exerted great influence, but who have been generally upstaged in the political arena by Boston's shrewd Irish politicians—the Curleys, McCormicks, Fitzgeralds, O'Neills and Kennedys.

On the whole, Boston is a mixture of communities, with sizeable Irish, Italian, Afro-American and Puerto Rican populations. Many of their ancestors came to the city to work in the leather-goods and textile mills, foundries and firearms factories that once made New England the leading manufacturer in the United States. Much of that industry is gone now.

The region has moved instead into the business world of high-technology electronics—with great success, particularly in and around the city of Bos-

1

ton. This new field has sprung from a magnificent seedbed of colleges and universities—among them some of the world's finest, such as Harvard and the Massachusetts Institute of Technology—that have been collecting in the area since before the United States came into existence. In the Boston area alone flourish more than 60 degree-granting institutions.

Despite the new industries and new people, there lingers in New England an adherence to the old-fashioned ways—and a stiff-backed contrariness about being told what to do. "Live free or die" is the motto stamped on New Hampshire number plates—produced, ironically, by the state's prison inmates. And not long ago, in an episode of Yankee revivalism, a New Hampshire town named Walpole took the risk of economic demise by voting against a proposal to permit the construction of a pulp mill, whose new jobs would have come at the perceived price of giving the town over to the mill.

Such individualism does not always mean rejecting something new. Not long ago, a meeting in the Vermont hamlet of Craftsbury was considering whether to create a fire-fighting district within part of the town, so that the town could raise capital on its own to salvage an ageing water facility. A voter who had recently moved to the area claimed that the proposal would change the "character" of Craftsbury. At that point a trusted old-timer stood up to say, "I've lived in Craftsbury all my life, and as long as I'm here, it won't change." The vote ran three to one against the newcomer and for the fire district. "You have to learn to be quiet when you first move into a small town," explained one woman.

Below New England lies the Middle

Atlantic Seaboard, an area of wealth, power and tremendous ethnic diversity. Nowhere are these qualities more evident than in New York City, the region's dynamo.

This roaring urban monster, with more than nine million residents in its metropolitan area (packed 24,700 to the square kilometre in the city's heart, Manhattan) pulses out its messages of commerce and entertainment to the whole earth. The New York stock exchanges trade the majority of all corporate shares publicly bought and sold in the U.S.; six of the nation's 10 biggest banks are based there; and the headquarters buildings of the nation's three biggest television networks—Columbia Broadcasting System (CBS), American Broadcasting Companies (ABC) and National Broadcasting Company (NBC)—are situated close by one another.

New York City attracts people from every corner of the globe: some 17.5 million tourists arrive annually, more than visit any other U.S. city, and gape upwards at the soaring skyscrapers.

For a long time it lured, as the country's principal port of entry, millions of immigrants, with the result that it became the most ethnically mixed of all the nation's cities.

Ukrainian-born taxi drivers joke with each other over their radios. The Central Park Mall hosts Italian opera in Korean. On Sixth Avenue, a busking West Indian steel-drum band plunks away for handouts. A Puerto Rican market flourishes in Spanish Harlem. Exuberant conversations in Greek are heard in coffee-houses in the section known as Astoria, while teenage gangs war tong-style in Manhattan's Chinatown. Up in Harlem and elsewhere, the city's black population struggles to break out of its cycle of low opportunity and low income, while in every part of the city the biggest urban concentration of Jews in the world—almost six times the number of citizens residing in Israel's twin cities of Tel Aviv-Jaffa—energizes the professions, commerce and the arts.

The atmosphere changes south of New York. The pace of life in Philadelphia, Pennsylvania, and Baltimore, Maryland, and their hinterlands is noticeably slower than in the larger metropolis to the north. And among the very rich who preside over the quiet elegance of estates along the Chesapeake Bay's shores and around Philadelphia there is an insistence upon understatement. A Philadelphia dowager who is directly descended from a signatory to the Declaration of Independence—and whose 32 grandchildren have each received from her more than $500,000—runs her own errands in a modest two-door car.

The climate, too, is softer here, the fields more fecund and more manicured, the hills lower, and the river estuaries braided with marshes full of game, fish and water birds. Perhaps the only time of noisy tension in rural Pennsylvania is mid-autumn, when thousands of deer hunters shoot up the woods with such a free hand that one old-timer pronounced himself "safer in the second battle of the Marne" than on a deer hunt outside the state capital of Harrisburg.

To the south of Pennsylvania is Washington, D.C., a federal enclave of tree-lined boulevards, imposing marble buildings and street drug dealers, of revered national monuments and boldly importuning prostitutes.

Washington employs 346,000 federal civilian workers and keeps many tens of thousands of other people busy in government-serving enterprises. So many of the government's activities involve legal questions that the city can claim roughly one lawyer for every 50 inhabitants, the highest ratio in the nation. (Washington also has more psychiatrists per capita than any other U.S. city.) In addition, the city attracts crowds of consultants and journalists as well as lobbyists, people who make a career of trying to influence the government on behalf of corporations or special-interest groups.

A majority of these lawyers, consultants and others who cluster round the government are white and they are all relatively well-off, many of them living in the suburbs of nearby Maryland or Virginia. The inhabitants of Washington itself are 70 per cent black and suffer chronic unemployment.

West of the Middle Atlantic Seaboard is the Great Lakes region, an area dedicated to production—in its enormous factories and clashing foundries. But steelmakers and other manufacturers fell on hard times in the late 1970s and early 1980s, as foreign competition and worldwide economic recession cut into their markets.

Shutdowns among the old, so-called smokestack industries of cities from Youngstown, Ohio, to Gary, Indiana, reversed a decades-long influx of job-seekers into the region. Some of the unemployed loaded their families and belongings into their cars and set off for jobs in the new high-technology and service industries that had sprung up in the South and South-west.

Still, America remains the world's

1

third largest steel producer and the world's leading manufacturer of cars. And the economy of the Mid-west, which includes the farming states of the central plains as well as the Great Lakes states, has a robust agricultural base, which ensures survival and even a measure of continued prosperity for most of the region.

The state of Iowa has built upon its farming wealth a cultural edifice that includes a renowned symphony orchestra at Des Moines and a highly regarded writers' workshop at the university. At an Iowa agricultural research centre, beneath a mural by Grant Wood, one of the country's great painters, is the motto, "When tillage begins, other arts follow." Apparently so. In the twin cities of Minneapolis–St. Paul, Minnesota, long America's flour-milling centre, more than a million tickets a year are sold for theatre, symphony and dance events.

In the heart of this vast region is the metropolis regarded by many people as the epitome of the nation's way of life: Chicago, Illinois. Poet Carl Sandburg described it as the "City of the Big Shoulders . . . Tool Maker, Stacker of Wheat, Player with Railroads and the Nation's Freight Handler. . . ." The location of Chicago was hardly inviting in the beginning—a boggy, insect-ridden piece of land on the shore of Lake Michigan. But the work-minded pioneers who first settled there did not care about the conditions.

Chicago today is America's leader in the production of steel, communications equipment, industrial machinery, household appliances and musical instruments. The city has three of the world's five tallest buildings, including the tallest, called the Sears Tower. Chicago also boasts O'Hare Airport, one of the busiest on earth, which sends at least 50 million passengers a year to more than 230 direct destinations. Only 11 nations in the world generate more services and goods than the city of Chicago.

For all the bustle and change, the Mid-west hangs on to its provincial ways. Like the prairie itself, the people tend to be more open and outgoing than those in the East. Iowa towns still hold social gatherings to make quilts. Any autumn Saturday afternoon, half the town of Lincoln, Nebraska, cheers the local football heroes, and on winter weekend nights, it seems all of Indiana is at a basketball game.

The people are also self-possessed. One day, Kansas City steak-house proprietor Arthur Bryant looked out of his modest establishment to behold a cavalcade of police and Secret Service cars—and the presidential limousine approaching his place. Out stepped then-Chief Executive Jimmy Carter, hungry for some good Kansas City beef. Betraying not even the slightest awe, Bryant greeted Carter with a line from an old popular song. "If I'd known you were coming," he joked, "I'd have baked a cake."

Below the Mid-west and the Middle Atlantic Seaboard is the South, whose attempt to secede from the rest of the United States led to the Civil War in the 1860s. Southerners still frequently refer to their region by its old nickname, Dixie, and they cherish their neighbourly, mannerly, easy-does-it, God-fearing traditions.

Here young boys are taught to stand up when a woman or an older man enters a room, and a question gets a smile and an answer that ends in "Sir" or "Ma'am". It is a place where a Mississippi farmer gets out of bed and into

A jagged skyline of recently built skyscrapers bespeaks the vitality of Chicago, Illinois, the Mid-west's biggest city. The showpiece is the pyramidal Hancock Tower, soaring 335 metres above Lakeshore Drive.

1

his pick-up at 2 a.m. on a rainy morning to carry a poor neighbour's sick child 50 kilometres to the nearest big hospital, then quietly pays the doctor himself, with the shy explanation later to the neighbour that there was no fee. Departing visitors, whether saying goodbye after a week with relatives or simply pulling away from a petrol station, hear the unvarying: "Y'all come back and see us—hear?" And the speaker means it.

Religion remains a strong force in the South. The Southern Baptist Convention is the largest and the wealthiest Protestant church group in the U.S. So strong is the hand of pleasure-denying fundamentalism that Moore County, Tennessee, where craftsmen lovingly distill Jack Daniel's bourbon whiskey, forbids the sale of any alcoholic spirits within its own borders.

Dixie remains defensive about its erstwhile prevalent attitudes towards the region's blacks, some 20 per cent of the population; many of the schools remained racially segregated for years after the U.S. Supreme Court declared the practice to be unconstitutional in 1954. One consequence of segregation and other racist practices was a massive exodus of blacks from the region, particularly the younger blacks, that began in the 1920s and continued through most of the 1960s.

In recent years, however, the so-called "black problem" has gradually ceased to be an all-consuming issue. In 1981, Mississippi—which only 10 years earlier had the smallest number of registered black voters in the United States—led the nation in the number of elected black officials. Attitudes towards race, along with many other things in the South, have undergone such change that the old Dixie lingers

more as an idea, an emotion, than as a monolithic region.

The new South is richly productive. It leads the nation in textile manufacturing, comes close in timber production and has such diverse industries as rubber and plastics, transportation equipment, petrochemicals and electrical parts. Cotton—once known as King Cotton to Southern farmers—has become but a consort to a newer, more valuable crop, soy beans.

High salaries paid to aerospace workers in Huntsville, Alabama, Houston, Texas, and Cape Canaveral, Florida, have helped to narrow the wage differential between the South and the rest of the nation. New Orleans, once known principally for its French heritage, Dixieland jazz and uninhibited Mardi Gras festival, has overlaid the smell of gumbo (a local dish made with shellfish, okra, ham, chicken and sassafras, among other ingredients) with that of oil from offshore drilling rigs in the Gulf of Mexico. Petroleum-tanker traffic has turned this city into the nation's busiest port.

Perhaps the most surprising aspect of all these changes is the composition of the South's population. Lately, many more blacks—most of them young and well educated—have been moving back into the region than have been leaving it. Like hundreds of thousands of South-bound whites, they are fleeing the high unemployment, high urban crime rate, pollution and cold winters of the North. Once again Dixie, now perhaps more widely known as the eastern arm of the Sun Belt, can proudly claim to be the land that provides people with a good living.

Texas used to be part of the Confederacy, and the state's people still sing the South's Civil War song, "Dixie".

COMEBACK OF AN INSTITUTION

Small-town America is sometimes described in elegiac terms—as a comfortable way of life overtaken by the present and about to vanish forever. In truth, it is very much alive across much of the U.S. and thriving. The 1980 census indicated that while the overall U.S. population grew by 4.8 per cent in the 1970s, towns of fewer than 2,500 inhabitants gained by 8.7 per cent and those of 2,500 to 25,000 by 7.5 per cent.

This rural resurgence is the result of several factors. More retired people with fixed incomes and the freedom to leave the high-priced cities and suburbs have fled to the country. Workers have followed their jobs into small towns as industries move out of inner cities into more remote areas, often in the Sun Belt. Others, tired of the hustle and bustle, the crime and grime of cities, have sought tranquillity in small towns.

One such refuge is Winterset, Iowa, population 4,000, located in rolling farmland 55 kilometres from Des Moines. Settled by Easterners in 1849, it still has seven covered bridges, plus a town square (right), a volunteer fire department, 12 churches, three schools and nine small manufacturing plants, one hospital, three nursing homes, a weekly newspaper and scores of community groups devoted to everything from gardens to ex-servicemen and women's concerns. Since 1970, its population has grown by 10 per cent.

Winterset, like many other U.S. small towns, may seem clannish, insular and dull to someone who needs a city's stimulation. But those who live there are compensated by a sense of belonging to a community that offers security and serenity—and a drugstore with a soda fountain.

Winterset's town square is bordered by 50 businesses, including a hair salon that offers California hairstyles. The square is crowded on Saturday mornings, when farmers and townspeople come here to shop.

A big business as well as a diversion for people living in or near Winterset, Madison County's livestock auction takes place at least once a week. The signs advertise Winterset companies serving local farmers.

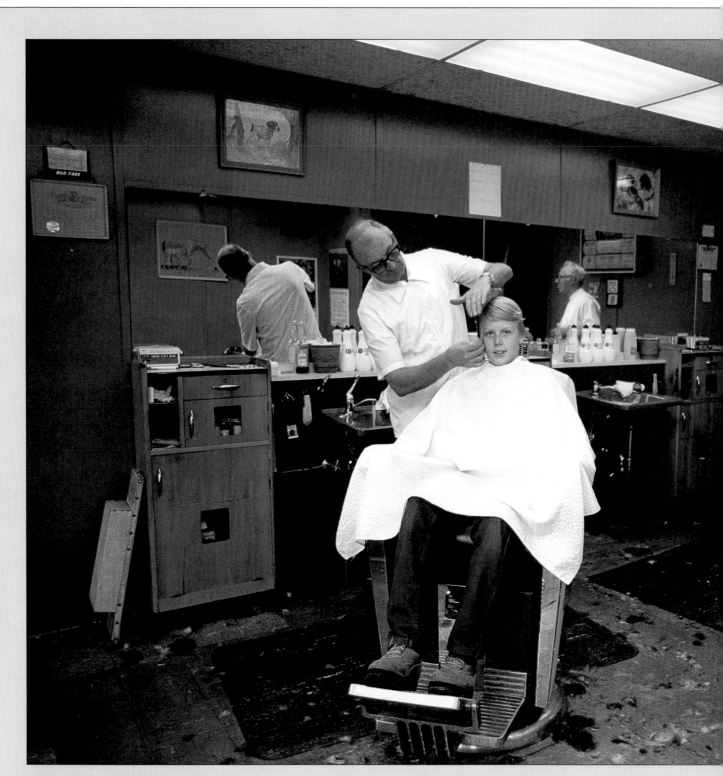

A male meeting place, the Northside Barber Shop serves more than 100 customers, plus the "regulars" who drop in for a daily chat.

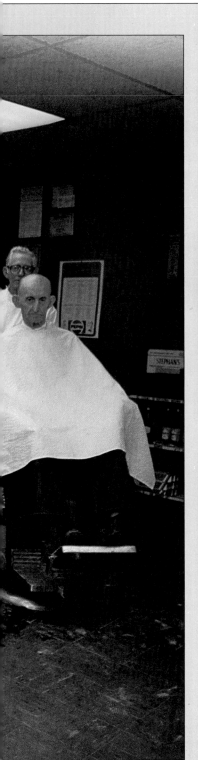

A favourite gathering spot is the 100-year-old Montross Pharmacy, where citizens come for coffee breaks and the soda fountain's home-made pies and cinnamon rolls.

The birthplace of Winterset's most famous native son is now a museum. Marion Morrison—screen name: John Wayne—was born in this house on May 26, 1907. His father was one of the town's pharmacists.

Erna Scherm plays the washboard for an elderly combo called the Hillbilly Band.

Marianne Fons *(left)* **and Liz Porter work on a quilt. Winterset women's favourite activities are both old and new—quilting and aerobics.**

33

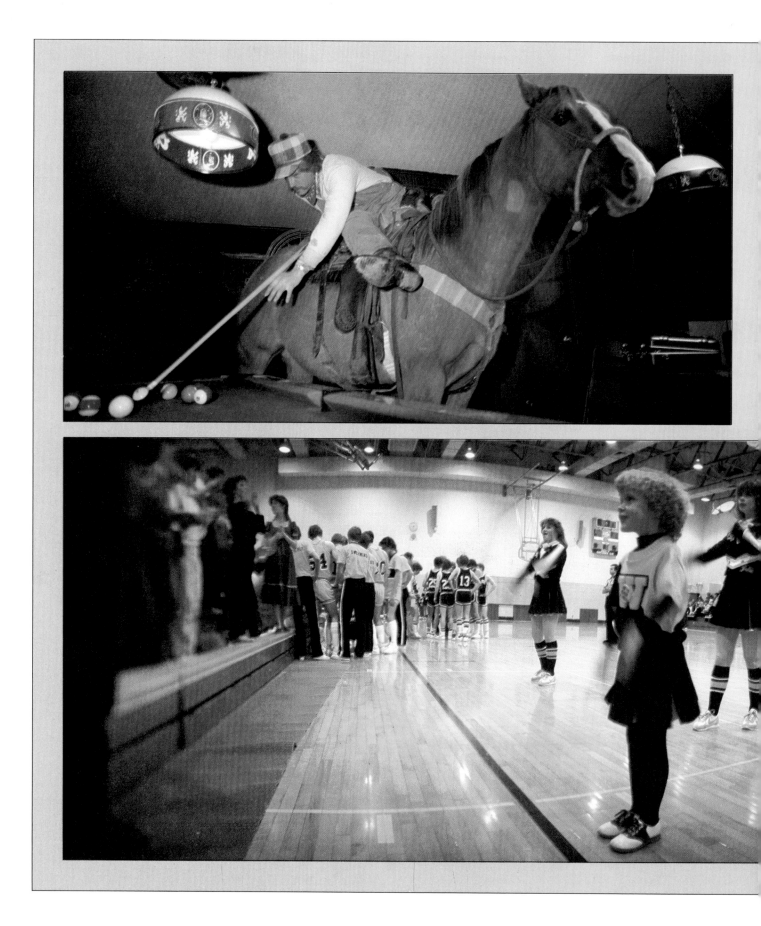

Winterset's most peculiar recreation is horseback pool. Matt Porter *(left)* and other local rodeo riders will clump into a tavern for a game; their horses usually get nervous, however, and have to be tethered outside while the game is finished on foot.

A more popular sport in the town is basketball; here the high school's Huskies take a break while the crowd responds to the cheerleaders, including the team's mascot, seven-year-old Angela Bass *(foreground)*.

But they sing "The Eyes of Texas" with more fervour, for this state is a region in itself, at least in spirit. Texas is a big place (its 691,027 square kilometres make it 25 per cent bigger in area than France), and most of its 14 million residents are proud of its size, its wealth and its rough-and-tumble frontier history.

Other Americans have not been so sure about Texas' charms. To many, the state's climate and countryside have represented a national nadir of parched soil, nasty winters (except along the coast) and worst of all, searingly hot and humid summers. Philip Sheridan, a Northern general in the Civil War, once remarked, "If I owned Texas and all Hell, I would rent out Texas and live in Hell."

But Texans have never paid much attention to anything said by people from anywhere else. Unlike their self-effacing Dixie neighbours, Texans are not afflicted by modesty. The residents of Dallas, who call their city "Big D", like to point out that the airport they share with nearby Fort Worth covers about the same amount of ground as all of Manhattan. They feel that their city is the natural habitat of the perennially slick and successful professional football team, the Dallas Cowboys, and of the team's perennially gorgeous cheerleaders. They are also gratified that Big D is home ground for what is probably the world's most expensive department store, Neiman-Marcus. There, a wealthy customer can pick up anything from a high-collared $100,000 sable coat to an exercise cycle that comes complete with a television screen and passing-scenery videotape.

The Dallas–Fort Worth area's population of three million is rivalled in Texas only by that of a booming sister metropolis, Houston, whose population had mushroomed by the early 1980s to 2.9 million. Houston, not far from the Gulf of Mexico, can be the hot and humid alternative to Hell that General Sheridan had in mind. But Houstonians, determined that they should make their city liveable and rich, keep comfortably cool by paying an annual air conditioning bill of close to a billion dollars. Much of this money comes from the offshore oil-drilling rigs in the Gulf of Mexico, whose lights wink above the horizon in the coastal haze of muggy summer nights. As all Texans will tell you, these wells have helped to ensure that their state is the nation's leading oil producer.

Today, more than 75 per cent of Texans live in these and other cities. Yet Texas' heart remains divided between its high-powered urban centres and its wide-open spaces. Despite all the braggadocio about big and new, so "down home", or countrified, does Texas profess to remain that its legislature officially presents the winner's title at the world championship chili-cooking contest staged annually in the little south-west Texan town of Terlingua. And so proud are Texans of their cowboy heritage that big-city youths who have never been on horseback commonly wear high-heeled boots and broad-brimmed Stetson hats and ride mechanical bucking bulls in bars they call honky-tonks. All Texan schoolchildren learn from an early age that their state was once (from 1836 to 1845) an independent republic.

A good deal of the state remains, indeed, not unlike the frontier of old. Outside the bounds of Houston's glitter and Dallas' moneyed urbanity, on the other side of a longitudinal boundary called the 100th meridian, lies a

1

much simpler Texas of large ranches and small, dusty towns. This Texas belongs to the seemingly endless, empty spaces of the great West. Beyond the 100th meridian the annual rainfall dwindles to 50 centimetres or less. All the way up the nation, cultivation is relatively easy to the east of this line. But to its west stretches short-grass country, where a steer needs 4 hectares or more to survive and where crops will not grow without irrigation from dams or wells, which have to go down 275 metres in places to reach water.

In this arid, 2,237,750-square-kilometre vastness that reaches from western Texas through Arizona and north to Montana—and is broken by the imposing spine of the Rocky Mountains—live fewer people than in the New York and Washington, D.C., metropolitan areas combined. Population density for the entire region is about 5 souls to the square kilometre—which means that, in a lot of places, you cannot even see your closest neighbour's house.

Moody relics of the region's history still lie scattered about: crumbled adobe walls, rusted mine machinery, zigzag slashes of mountain road going nowhere. In the northern Rockies the grass-grown ruts of the 19th-century Oregon Trail are still visible, so deeply were they cut by pioneer wagons. Wild horses, bighorn sheep and antelopes continue to inhabit the region's deserts, sagebrush plains and mountains. The place names evoke the past: Wolf Point, Cheyenne Wells, Mule Shoe and Broken Bow.

This huge territory has never appeared very hospitable. In 1821 Major Stephen Long, who led an expedition into what he then named the Great American Desert, pronounced the land "almost wholly unfit for cultivation and of course, uninhabitable". Indeed, were it not for the determination and the genius of the people who came after, it would still be that. Dry in summer, the high plains of Montana can be so cold in the winter months that during blizzards healthy Hereford cattle are likely to freeze to death where they stand. "It's a deceitful country, hard, mean, with floods and droughts and tornadoes," said one resident. "But look at it," he added. "God Almighty, it's so beautiful."

Farmers who settled the southern and central Great Plains adopted hardy Russian winter wheat, which can grow in the dry conditions. To the north they planted spring wheat, which is ready for harvest before the advent of the area's early, severe winters. As a result, significant stretches of what was once wasteland today make up one of the world's major cereal-producing regions.

One of the most striking achievements was the transformation of the land around Utah's Great Salt Lake, which Indians avoided because of its saline sterility. Here, in the mid-19th century, the Mormons, members of an austere theocratic society, chose to live where they would not be bothered, and to make something out of nothing. Gouging out canals and constructing dams in the snowfields of the neighbouring Wasatch Mountains and also developing large scale irrigation methods, they turned the Salt Lake flats into a thriving metropolitan area of almost a million people living amid broad swaths of greenery.

Lately, the cities of this part of the West have experienced an exponential growth. One reason is the climate: the southern portion of the region lies in the same Sun Belt that encompasses Dixie and that since the 1960s has grown in population more rapidly than any other part of the country. A second factor that has helped turn the old cow towns and Spanish mission centres such as Albuquerque, New Mexico, into modern metropolises has been the West's extraordinary mineral and energy reserves.

Another, paradoxical attraction of this essentially spartan environment has been recreation and leisure. Over the years the federal government has incorporated 29.8 million hectares nationwide into the National Park System, and some of the largest and most spectacular parks of the U.S. are in the West. The government, in fact, owns almost 50 per cent of all the land west of the 100th meridian. Millions of tourists annually visit such spectacular national parks as Yellowstone, Bryce Canyon, Grand Teton and Grand Canyon, as well as hundreds of other, smaller parks.

But for many Americans, another region is probably even more exciting—and surely more naturally alluring. That is the Pacific states, which include California, Oregon, Washington, Hawaii and gigantic Alaska. Here is America's own promised land, the region to which Americans themselves have emigrated.

Hawaii lies a third of the way across the Pacific Ocean. In some ways it is the paradise it advertises itself to be. Made up of volcanic islands and coral atolls, the state sits just within the balmy northern rim of the tropics. Down from the mountain peaks on all the islands tumbles a profusion of tropical vegetation—lush ferns, brilliant hibiscus and stately palms. The sandy beaches and rolling surf of Hawaii are legend-

ary. Naturally, tourism is one of the state's biggest industries.

Given such endowments, it is a wonder the islands have not long since been submerged by mass migrations from mainland America. One deterrent, however, is the lack of habitable space. So mountainous are the islands that almost all of the state's 965,000 people are to be found in the small, easternmost segments of Hawaii's 16,640-square-kilometre area.

Caucasians constitute about a third of the population. The islands' original inhabitants were Polynesians, who were ravaged by diseases brought by missionaries, whalers and other early sojourners. Today they constitute less than 1 per cent of all Hawaiians. The rest are a remarkable mix, mainly descendants of immigrants from Japan, the Philippines and China.

Hawaii has the nation's highest pro-portion of interracial marriages. The Caucasians tend to marry other Caucasians, and the Japanese still tend to marry other Japanese; for the remaining ethnic groups, however, more than half of all the marriages are made outside the group.

Both climate and opportunity—as well as the landscape—are wholly different in Alaska, which sprawls over an incredible 1,478,450 square kilometres; the United Kingdom, West Germany, France and Italy together could fit into it with space left over. Alaskan living is hard, and winter temperatures can plunge to −50°C. There are few roads, and distances between places are so huge that most towns have to be supplied by sea or air. Fewer than half a million people have settled in this enormous space, 40 per cent in and around the coastal city of Anchorage. For determined individuals, however, chances to make good abound.

Alaska holds the largest oil reserve in North America, near Prudhoe Bay on the Arctic coast. From there the oil is pumped through a 1,287-kilometre pipeline running south to the year-round ice-free port of Valdez. In the 1970s, a lorry driver or labourer working in the oilfields or along the pipeline could earn an income equal to that of a successful executive based in New York. And although the cost of living is high in this air-lift economy, there is spare cash in Alaska—literally for everyone: in a period of several months in 1982 and 1983, the oil-glutted state gave a dividend of $1,000 to every adult state resident.

The people of the Pacific North-west states—Washington and Oregon—flourish on another kind of bonus. Whereas much of Alaska is cold through most of the year, the relatively

1

mild though moist climate of Washington and Oregon pervades a countryside that looks like a real-life replica of an idealized landscape painting. Within sight of central Portland and Seattle rise snow-capped mountains. Lakes and protected bays have spawned hundreds of thousands of pleasure craft around Seattle alone.

The mighty Columbia River, forming some three fourths of the border between the two states, provides low-cost power for homes and industries. In the 1930s, the federal government began damming the river: the Grand Coulee, the Bonneville and 24 other dams in the system are the heart of a North-west network that generates 43 per cent of all the hydroelectric power in the nation.

Recent opinion surveys concluded that Seattle and Portland are the two "most liveable" cities in the United States. Seattle's location between Puget Sound and Cascade Range makes it possible in summer for an outdoor enthusiast to sail, water-ski and then ski on the slopes close by—all in one exhilarating day.

With fewer available jobs to attract Americans compared to California to the south, the North-west has not seen the influx of people that has made California the country's most populous state, home for 23 million people. California leads the nation in production of goods and services (were it an independent country, it would rank seventh in the world in gross national product). But Californians also spend a lot of time and energy in leisure activities.

This is the land of surfboards, hot tubs *(pages 40–41)* and Hollywood's Sunset Strip nightclubs. It was the birthplace of the 1960s hippie culture and, almost certainly, is America's top consumer of illegal "recreational drugs"; a fun-and-sun-loving state of endless golden beaches.

The traveller and author John Gunther wrote of California that its

Children explore the crumbling edge of Portage Glacier, a river of ice that flows into Prince William Sound in south-central Alaska. The state has hundreds of glaciers, covering about 30 per cent of the land.

"climate is worshipped as a god". But also revered are money, fame, the perfection of the human body and the nebulous notions of self-awareness and self-fulfilment.

The state of California contains two of the most fascinating cities in the United States, San Francisco and Los Angeles (recognized throughout the world by its initials: L.A.). San Francisco may well be the country's best-loved city; many Americans list it on opinion polls as their favourite or at least as second-favourite, after their own birthplace. It may, indeed, be America's most beautiful. San Francisco gleams and sparkles on a hilly peninsula between the Pacific Ocean and San Francisco Bay, and the city's most famous landmark, the Golden Gate Bridge, soars across the narrows dividing the two bodies of water.

San Francisco is a city that never stops looking at itself, since its neighbourhoods of boldly coloured Victorian houses climb the sides and rise from the peaks of its 43 hills, offering countless stunning, irresistible views.

From San Francisco a road winds 700 kilometres south to Los Angeles along one of the world's most breathtaking coastlines, where sheer cliffs drop into the pounding Pacific surf below. An inland route cuts through California's agricultural heart, the great Central Valley, home of the state's wine industry and its huge agribusiness concerns. Here, too, some remarkable sights can be seen: when farming machines switch on their headlights at dusk, they appear to be gigantic, glowing-eyed insects lumbering across the flat, fertile fields.

Newcomers driving to L.A. are never quite certain when they have reached the place. The municipal boundaries of

Off the shore of the Hawaiian island of Maui, a wind-surfer swoops down the face of a wave. Heavy Pacific swells make Hawaii a surfer's heaven. The native Polynesians were already enjoying the sport when the islands were discovered in 1778.

the city encompass only a small portion—1,200 square kilometres—of the metropolis generally known by the name of Los Angeles. Most of the urban complex lies within the 10,575 square kilometres of Los Angeles County, but many of the 11.5 million people who for all practical purposes are Angelenos actually reside in various parts of the four adjacent counties.

Built in an arid region, it is necessary for Los Angeles to import almost all of its water, some from as far as 400 kilometres away. From nature's standpoint, this may be the unlikeliest spot on earth for a great city to have been

established, and nature at times seems determined to prove it.

Probably no other urban centre in the world is threatened by so many natural disasters. Waves driven by Pacific Ocean storms occasionally smash expensive houses built along the shores of Los Angeles' coastal communities, and mudslides caused by torrential rain frequently tumble other residences from their precarious hillside perches. Every few years, forest fires fanned by hot, dry winds that come in from the desert destroy millions of dollars' worth of homes. (What other city on earth is plagued by forest fires?)

A STATE WITH ITS OWN LIFESTYLE

"What we want the whole country to be," an ex-governor of California once said, "California already is." It leads the United States in farm income. It has the greatest concentration of high-technology industries in the world and 30 per cent of all the U.S. aeronautical engineers; one Californian in 10 has a college degree. At the same time, the state is the centre of antitechnology activities and proud of its ecological regulations. Above all, it is the trend-setter for the American lifestyle.

California represents "absolute freedom, mobility and privacy . . . the instinct which drove America to the Pacific," wrote Californian native and author Joan Didion. Of all the fads and movements that have influenced the country, more have arisen in California than in any other state.

From this benign climate came the ideal of the indoor-outdoor home—roof gardens, balconies, terraces, houseboats, patios and, more recently, hot tubs *(below)*. Here is the fountainhead of surfing, backpacking (hiking), all-day roller skating, the shopping centre, suburban sprawl and life lived in

Photographer Michael Powers *(right)*, **his daughter Marika and friends relax in Powers' hot tub—one of some 500,000 owned by Americans—nea**

the car. California has drive-in churches as well as drive-in supermarkets.

But California is not only a source of the new; it is also a goal. It is "the last stop," wrote Joan Didion, "for all those who came from somewhere else, for all those who have drifted away from the cold and the past and the old ways."

e home he built south of San Francisco.

Then there is the ever-present threat of earthquakes, which Los Angeles shares with San Francisco. Both lie perilously close to one of the earth's great geological rifts, the San Andreas Fault. Los Angeles suffers numerous earth tremors, including one not so long ago that was strong enough to bring down motorway flyovers. Meanwhile, earthquake experts, as well as Angelenos and San Franciscans, await what they refer to as "the big one", a quake of cataclysmic proportions.

People and their cars do their share to increase the hazards and harassments of life in L.A. There are an incredible 5.3 million motor vehicles in Los Angeles County alone, one for every 1.4 persons. Motor exhaust fumes are the principle contributor to the city's notorious smog, a chemical haze that hangs suffocatingly over the Los Angeles basin most days, bringing tears to stinging eyes.

But Angelenos would not—indeed, could not—do without their cars. L.A. has sometimes been called a city in search of a centre, because until fairly recently it lacked a definable central area. Now it has many "downtowns" scattered throughout the metropolis, each a concentration of high-rise commercial buildings. All four corners of Los Angeles County are linked together by 640 kilometres of conventional roads and motorways and 800 kilometres of dual carriageways called "freeways"—a glaring misnomer when standstill traffic jams snarl the system during rush hours. Public transportation is minimal: for all practical purposes, there is no other way to get around than by car.

Anyway, the Angelenos love their cars. No amount of smog could stop film moguls from swanning about in

their Rolls-Royces—although one distinctly L.A. phenomenon has put at least a small snag in that flaunting of wealth: motorized muggers who follow Rolls drivers home in order to rob them in their driveways.

And, it would seem, Los Angeles cannot offer enough urban problems, either natural or man-made, to prevent more people and more cars from going there. That is not truly puzzling, however, because nature has blessed the place with almost year-round warmth and its people have made it an exciting and economically thriving city. Moreover, the ubiquitous car puts almost all of L.A.'s residents within a couple of hours' reach of snow-clad mountains in one direction and the sandy Pacific beaches in another.

As befits the ultimate city of a nation of immigrants, most of the newcomers to Los Angeles lately have been of foreign origin. Since 1970, more than two million immigrants have settled in the city, leading one demographer to liken Los Angeles to the old immigrant-processing facility which operated in New York Bay: "There's no question that it is the new Ellis Island."

The new arrivals have come mainly from Pacific-rim nations such as El Salvador, Mexico, the Philippines, Taiwan, Vietnam and Korea. As recently as 1960, only one in nine Los Angeles County residents was Hispanic, and just one in 100 was of Asian descent. By the early 1980s, almost a third of the country's 7.9 million population was Hispanic and a 10th was Asian. Whites made up less than half the population, which meant that *everybody* living in Los Angeles County was a member of a minority group. It would be difficult to conceive of a more American situation than that.

LOVE AFFAIR WITH THE OPEN ROAD

To drive across the United States on one of its many motorways is to know how the nation lives—forever in motion. Founded by people on the move, America has grown up as the most mobile country on earth, its inhabitants travelling by train, by plane, but most of all in roaring streams of motor vehicles such as those on the right. In America, where some six million kilometres of paved roads carry an awesome total of 156 million cars, lorries and buses, the open road means far more than simply transportation.

Every day of their lives, most Americans spend at least some time on the road. What other nation would build 40,000 motels, sell billions of hamburgers from roadside fast-food chains, or pick up its alcoholic beverages at drive-through liquor stores?

The road that may best reveal the U.S. character is Interstate 80, a double ribbon stretching 5,000 kilometres from coast to coast with not one stop light. Starting with the grumble of Manhattan's commuters, I-80 plunges through the heart of Middle America—gritty mill towns and tiny islands of horse-drawn America—to climax in a sweep of plains and mountains leading to San Francisco Bay.

A stacked road sign on Interstate 80, a main artery of the 68,500-kilometre, 56-billion-dollar U.S. motorway system, offers a compelling invitation to a restless nation in love with its cars.

The George Washington Bridge carries dawn traffic over the Hudson between New York City and Fort Lee, New Jersey, I-80's eastern starting-point.

1

2

3

1 Wearing the railwayman's traditional cap, an engineer peers from the cab window of a diesel locomotive rolling alongside Interstate 80 at Paterson, New Jersey, 32 kilometres west of the George Washington Bridge.

2 A brightly coloured van carries bread into the Pennsylvanian countryside from a central bakery in Easton, Pennsylvania. Across the U.S., vehicles such as this and articulated lorries haul more than a billion and a half tonne-kilometres of freight every year.

3 A cosy antique shop in Stroudsburg, Pennsylvania, displays its potpourri of quilts, pillows, spices, dolls and children's clothes. A quiet resort town, Stroudsburg nestles 5 kilometres from the spectacular Delaware Water Gap, which cleaves the wooded Kittatinny Mountains.

4 Tendrils of smoke trail away from the stacks and towers of a steel plant along Ohio's Mahoning River. In one stretch along its banks, mills and Bessemer converters stand cheek-by-jowl for a distance of more than 30 kilometres.

5 Two steelworkers stroll out of the gate of a mill in Youngstown, Ohio, after finishing work. Skilled hands such as these produce a third of the world's steel, and 15 per cent of all their output goes into America's motor vehicles.

6 A Chicago barman in a bar like thousands of others along I-80 smiles behind the barrier that distances him from his customers, enabling him to perform the barman's time-honoured role of listener.

The Great Falls at Paterson, New Jersey, boom between the frames of a venerable bridge and some modern graffiti. The first planned industrial town in the United States, Paterson was laid out in 1791 by the statesman Alexander Hamilton.

4

5

6

1   An Amish mother in Indiana, clad in the old-fashioned bonnet and other plain clothing required by her religious sect, a branch of the Mennonites, adjusts the mantle of a gas lamp. The Amish shun most modern trappings, but may compromise on appliances such as stoves and refrigerators.

2   A covered bridge on a snowy side road near the motorway, in Madison County, Iowa, is preserved as a reminder of the days when people travelled by horse and buggy and sheltered under its long roof when caught out in a storm.

3   Iowa livestock-raiser George Mueller chortles happily as he embraces a stuffed bison (also called buffalo) head and the decorated skull of a longhorn cow. Although he specializes in cattle, Mueller also grazes bison, whose wild ancestors used to roam the West by the tens of millions.

4   A postbox whose support has been cut and painted to represent Uncle Sam stands in the snow outside a timber-frame house in Iowa, in the farm country that stretches into the rich prairie on either side of I-80.

5   Two University of Nebraska students play pinball and video games in the Student Union recreation room in Lincoln, capital of Nebraska. From Lincoln to the Pacific, I-80 runs parallel to the route of America's first transcontinental railway.

6   Scout's Rest, in Nebraska, served as the winter quarters of Buffalo Bill Cody, the one-time Indian-fighter whose Wild West Show toured the world in the late 19th and early 20th centuries. He once slaughtered 4,000 buffaloes in the area over 17 months.

7   A massive grain elevator towers above the one and two-storey buildings in Gothenburg, Nebraska—named after the Swedish city by the Scandinavians who led the migration of Northern and Central Europeans to the region.

5   6   7

Amish buggies, still the prescribed means of everyday travel for their owners, stand near a barn in LaGrange, Indiana. In the mid-19th century, thousands of Amish came to the Mid-west from farms in Pennsylvania.

47

1 2 3

1 Parked just off I-80 in Wyoming, articulated lorries await their drivers outside a McDonald's fast-food stop, whose golden-arch insignia can be seen above the cab of the most distant lorry.
2 A proud driver taking a break from the road shows off a T-shirt caricaturing his trade. Two-way citizens'-band radios and even husband-wife driving teams have alleviated the boredom of long-haul driving.
3 The symbol of a cowboy riding a bucking horse on the number plate of a Wyoming vehicle announces that this is cattle country. Second in the West only to Montana for livestock breeding, Wyoming has 1,400,000 head of cattle and fewer than 500,000 people.
4 The Eagle Gate, a landmark on State Street in Salt Lake City, Utah, frames the Utah State Capitol building. Rising in the distance are the Wasatch Mountains, whose winter snow cover provides virtually all the water for this thriving desert city of 160,000.
5 The brilliantly lighted Mormon Temple, focal point for the Church of Jesus Christ of Latter-day Saints, rises above the trees of Temple Square in the heart of Salt Lake City. Devout, energetic and prosperous, Mormons traditionally send their young adults on two-year missions across the United States and overseas.
6 Minnie Dick, a Western Shoshoni woman, works at handicrafts in her home on the South Fork Indian Reserve along Nevada's Humboldt River. Rising in snow-capped mountains, the Humboldt grows shallow and disappears in the sand and clay of Nevada's desert interior.

4   5   6

A handful of mixed range cattle stare towards the road from a field of sagebrush and snow. On the high plains of the West it takes 4 hectares of such sparse land to sustain a single steer.

1 Not far from I-80, a petrol station in the backwater of Golconda, Nevada, crouches forlornly in the late afternoon sun, its sign empty and its water tower a skeleton of girders.

2 A "hurry-up" wedding chapel in Reno, Nevada, adorned with neon hearts, awaits its bustling trade. Though more famed for gambling and for divorces that require only six weeks' state residence, Reno annually sees eight times as many weddings take place as marriages sundered.

3 Ghost-town resident Louise Buckingham plays with two cats clinging to a picket fence in the mud and melting snow of Paradise Valley, Nevada. She lives in the remains of the town hotel with her husband, Fred—whose father, a prospector, founded the town around the turn of the century.

4 This snowbound cemetery holds former inhabitants of another Nevada ghost town, Tuscarora, north of I-80. The high plains and mountains of the West are spotted with abandoned towns and mines, the residuum of gold and silver strikes during the 19th and early 20th centuries.

5 A Lake Tahoe resident blasts his snowmobile through the winter forest. Such vehicles are here—as elsewhere—actively discouraged by environmentalists, who object to exhaust pollution and the disruption of wildlife in the ecologically fragile mountain region.

6 A waitress serves up drinks at a Lake Tahoe restaurant, on the border between California and Nevada. Many such young women double as ski instructors during the area's five-month winter-sports season in the surrounding mountains.

7 An icicle-draped motel stands isolated in the snowy heights of the Sierra. The clientele includes gamblers and senior citizens who stay here for Lake Tahoe's casinos and night life.

4   5   6   7

The westbound lane of I-80 stretches string-straight to the horizon of Nevada's snow-speckled desert land. Since 1960, the U.S. has spent $20 billion on building and maintaining its motorways—more than on anything else except defence.

1
2
3

1 A bright haze hangs above the water on the California shore of Lake Tahoe. More than two thirds of the 35-kilometre-long, 19-kilometre-wide lake lies within California; the remainder is in the state of Nevada.

2 Skiers tired from a day on the slopes of the High Sierra wallow in the hot water and steam of a whirlpool bath. There are about 10 major ski resorts within 30 kilometres of Donner Pass, where I-80 cuts between peaks 3,000 metres high.

3 A green landscape near the Napa Valley, a leading wine-producing region, contrasts dramatically with the ski country only a few kilometres to the east. Such geographic variance is characteristic of California, where subarctic mountain peaks, hot desert areas and temperate enclaves adjoin.

4 Oil tanks line the motorway as I-80 nears California's coastal range. Some of America's largest oil deposits lie in California and its offshore fields, giving the state an annual oil production of 385 million barrels.

5 A modified triangular-frame country home, with a private aeroplane parked outside, nestles amid the rounded hills of the coastal mountains. Property has long been a prime investment in California, where an influx of newcomers helps to boost sales.

6 Three bearded, beaded young men pass a bemused onlooker in San Francisco's Haight-Ashbury district. The city's population is a microcosm of cosmopolitan California—wealthy business people, Asian families, Italian fishermen, Hispanic émigrés, university people and a restless legacy of hippies from the 1960s.

4

5

6

On the final kilometre of its journey from the East Coast, I-80 soars grandly upon the Oakland Bay Bridge, alight in the early evening, with the city of San Francisco in the background.

Abraham Lincoln's craggy visage
receives an unceremonious bath to
remove accumulated grime. More
than three million visitors a year
come to see the marble statue in
Washington D.C.'s Lincoln Memorial.

SEEKING A MORE PERFECT UNION

The tension is still there in the faded words on parchments preserved in the glass cases of the National Archives. First, the Declaration of Independence. It is unequivocal and direct. "All men" have "unalienable Rights," it says, to "Life, Liberty and the pursuit of Happiness." Government exists to secure those benefits—and when it fails to do so, the people have the right "to abolish it, and to institute new Government." There is no mistaking the noise in the background: the sound of guns making a revolution.

In another display case is a document that begins, "We the People of the United States, in Order to form a more perfect Union, establish Justice, insure domestic Tranquillity ... and secure the blessings of Liberty ... do ordain and establish this Constitution ..." In contrast, this document is talking about creating a government, not abolishing one, about nailing down liberty by restricting it in some essential ways. Absolute liberty must have its boundaries in order to guarantee union, justice and "Tranquillity", a word that is intriguingly different from the Declaration's "Happiness".

Liberty and order, the individual's pursuit of happiness, the society's quest for tranquillity: these are the sometimes conflicting aims that the American people have been attempting to reconcile during more than two centuries of tremendous growth and change. The history of the United States, has been, and it continues to be, a non-stop balancing act between abstract ideals and pragmatic needs.

The debate over the rival claims of liberty and order goes back to the very seedtime of the nation. By 1634, ten thousand of the English religious dissidents known as Puritans had established a colony in Massachusetts. Their leader was a successful lawyer, John Winthrop, who had forsaken his comfortable estate in order to worship God in the wilderness as he saw fit. He endorsed the Puritan notion that a proper society was one governed by magistrates, chosen by male church members. To them alone God would reveal his ideas of proper administration. All others would be "free" to obey the government of God's servants.

Even for some Massachusetts Puritans, that was too strong a medicine. Roger Williams, though a clergyman, was wary of uniting the powers of church and state. What would happen, he asked, when reasonable people disagreed on God's meaning? If one side used the authority of government to beat down its opponents, that would be just like the tyranny from which they had all tried to escape. Williams wanted to let people alone in matters of conscience, and for everyone a share in rule. Governments, he contended, should have "no more power than the people shall betrust them with."

Massachusetts leaders voted Williams out of the colony in 1635. A few

2

years later they did the same to the first of a long procession of strong-minded Yankee women, Anne Hutchinson, whom Winthrop uncharitably labelled "the American Jezebel". Apparently, her sin was to argue that God might hint his intentions directly to an individual believer (either male or female) rather than only to the magistrates. Williams and Hutchinson and their exiled followers founded a new colony, Rhode Island, where the separation of church and state was eventually guaranteed by law.

Williams' experiment in democracy was the exception, at least for a time. Other early colonies along North America's Atlantic Coast were established by companies or proprietors chartered by the English Crown. They were intended to make a profit for investors, and they were not meant to be run democratically. They were instead to be administered by authorities based in London. But geographical and historical logic pushed the English colonies towards wanting their liberty and self-government. For one thing, high-handed rule by proprietors or royal officials was likely to discourage any settlers, who had to be enticed to face the hardships of the wilderness by the promise of having a measure of freedom to run their own affairs (the glaring exceptions were African slaves, who were being brought into the Southern colonies as early as 1619).

For another, many of the English newcomers had lived through a period of struggle between king and parliament that was capped in 1689 by the enactment of British laws that included such guarantees as trial by jury, no taxation without the consent of parliament, and immunity from arbitrary seizure of property. When the heirs to

this parliamentary revolution travelled overseas, they expected that these hard-won "rights of freeborn Englishmen" would be theirs in the new land, or they would not go at all.

On paper, the English colonies still appeared to be run from London by administrators who possessed autocratic powers. But the truth was that by 1760 they were close to being self-governing republics, with colonial assemblies in which different factions fought legislative battles over who should benefit from the implementation of land, tax, currency and trade policies.

The British government proceeded unwittingly to make a nation out of these disparate political communities by an ill-considered attempt to tighten up imperial administration. King George III issued proclamations, and in parliament various acts were passed between 1763 and 1775 designed to raise revenue through new taxes, to enforce rules against smuggling and to prevent settlers from moving westwards, encroaching on Indian territory and provoking Indian wars. The British government, unaware of how strongly the colonists would resent the imposition of such edicts, was scarcely prepared for the resulting tidal wave of outraged reaction.

From Boston to Charleston, the colonists denounced such interference as positively un-English, submitting petitions ringing with determination that freeborn Britons should not be made slaves. They organized themselves and staged boycotts, demonstrations and riots—and when the British cracked down on them with tough new enforcement policies in 1775, resistance turned into revolution. A representative body, the Continental Congress, with members drawn from all of the 13

colonies, met in Philadelphia and took on the job of running a war.

Even while the guns were blazing away, many colonists continued to hope that their gracious sovereign would grant them autonomy within the Empire. But as it became evident that King George was quite willing to allow his red-coated troops to shoot down his overseas subjects, colonial resolve to be independent stiffened. Minds were changed, too, by Thomas Paine's best-selling 1776 pamphlet "Common Sense". Paine, who had come over from England only two years earlier, described George III as "the royal brute of Great Britain". He argued that "in free countries the law ought to be king; and there ought to be no other." The one-time colonists should transform themselves into "the FREE AND INDE-PENDENT STATES OF AMERICA".

The Continental Congress embraced that idea and shortly expressed it in the more formal terms of the Declaration of Independence. Five more years of hard fighting were needed to win the war and make the claim of independence good. In 1782, Britain agreed to a peace treaty. The 13 former British outposts became the United States of America. Loosely united under a concord called the Articles of Confederation, the Americans grappled with the question of how to govern themselves.

Were they now a single people requiring a single government, or was America an association of independent states? A strong central government was probably necessary to win respect and security in the world, but might it not swallow up the liberties it was supposed to protect? What liberties ought to be protected, anyway, and whose?

These were the fundamental issues faced by the 55 men who gathered in

Philadelphia in the spring of 1787 to revise and "improve" the Articles of Confederation, and ended up instead writing the Constitution. They were a remarkably well-educated group, predominantly young, but heavily experienced in pragmatic politics. Almost all of them, including the "Federalists" who argued the case for strengthening central government, had learnt to be suspicious of power, because of King George's heavy-handed use of it. And even those who spoke for light controls on the popular will recognized that individuals were mainly moved by self-interest and could not always be trusted to bear in mind the common good.

What they contrived was a set of compromises that divided power between the states and a strong central government. This would be checked by a theoretically equal division of authority between executive, legislative and judicial branches *(page 118)*. Even so, anti-federalists believed that the document handed over too much control to the government.

To meet such objections, the first U.S. Congress in its first regular session in 1789 fashioned 10 constitutional amendments, the Bill of Rights, which limited governmental power. These clauses confronted the government with a series of "thou shalt nots". Thou shalt not interfere with the free exercise of religion or speech. Thou shalt not deny trial by jury, nor engage in unreasonable searches of the people's dwellings or possessions. Thou shalt not claim any authority not specifically spelt out in the Constitution; all powers not mentioned there are "reserved to the states . . . or to the people".

The Constitution, at least until the Bill of Rights was added, was not quite democratic enough for free-thinking Thomas Jefferson, but he accepted it as the best that could be achieved at the time. It was too democratic for conservative New York lawyer Alexander Hamilton, but he, too, would settle for it as an attainable half loaf. These two men were brilliant exponents of totally opposed views of America's meaning. That both of them were able to work within the Constitution's deliberately open-ended framework is the best illustration of how superbly flexible and well-wrought the document was.

Jefferson was the first of a breed of patrician democrats, privileged Americans who embraced popular ideals. He was an uncommon defender of commoners—a planter, musician, surveyor, architect, lawyer and inventor, who held that government was best when it governed least. He was suspicious of the tendency of all governments to usurp and abuse power and believed that a rebellion by the people

A CHRONOLOGY OF KEY EVENTS

15,000–10,000 B.C. The first inhabitants of the New World arrive in Alaska via the Bering Strait, and spread down and across the Americas.

1500 B.C.–1500 A.D. Cultures arise among the peoples Christopher Columbus would misname "Indians".

c. 1000 Viking Chief Leif Erikson explores the North American east coast.

1565 Spanish explorers found St. Augustine, Florida, the first permanent European settlement.

1607 Jamestown, Virginia, the first permanent English colony, is founded.

1619 Virginia elects the first legislative assembly. The first blacks—20 indentured servants—arrive.

1620 Pilgrims arrive aboard the *Mayflower*; they establish a colony at Plymouth, Massachusetts.

1636 Harvard, the first college in the Colonies, is founded.

1664 The British seize New Amsterdam and rename it New York. Maryland's "black code" declares all blacks in the colony to be slaves for life.

1675–1678 King Philip's War: New England Indians attack settlements, trying to halt expansion by Europeans.

1682 French explorer Robert Cavalier de la Salle claims the Mississippi River valley with all its tributaries for France, naming the vast territory of Louisiana after King Louis XIV.

1704 The first regular newspaper, *Boston News Letter*, appears.

1754 At the Albany Congress, Benjamin Franklin uses the slogan "Join or Die" *(above)* to draw support for his Plan of Union, designed to protect the colonists' mutual interests. Although the plan is not ratified, it presages the federal union.

1755–1763 French and Indian War. At the end, France gives up possessions in the Ohio and Mississippi River valleys.

1764 Parliament's Revenue Act to tax colonists; boycott of imported items.

1767 More taxes are levied by parliament, including one on tea. Colonial protests and boycotts spread.

1770 The Boston Massacre; five people are killed by British troops.

1773 The cargo of an East India Company ship is thrown overboard at the Boston Tea Party *(above)*.

1774 English ships blockade Boston harbour; parliament annuls the Massachusetts government charter. The First Continental Congress issues a Declaration of Rights, calling for civil disobedience.

1775 Minutemen engage advancing British troops at Lexington and Concord *(below)*. The Second Continental Congress appoints George Washington Commander-in-Chief.

1681 Quaker William Penn founds Pennsylvania, which offers religious liberty under its progressive Charter of Privileges *(above)*.

1765 The Stamp Act goes into effect and violent opposition to it breaks out. Radical groups called Sons of Liberty are formed.

1776 The Declaration of Independence is approved on July 4.

1777–1780 Colonial forces win key battles. In 1777 the Stars and Stripes replaces a temporary flag that had incorporated the Union Jack.

1781 British General Charles Cornwallis, besieged at Yorktown by Washington's forces and their French allies, surrenders his entire army.

1787 The North-West Ordinance establishes procedures by which territories can become states.

1789 The Constitution is ratified and Washington is elected President. The first Congress meets. The Supreme Court is established.

1791 The first 10 amendments of the Constitution, known as the Bill of Rights, are put into effect.

1803 The western boundary of the U.S. is advanced to the Rocky Mountains with the purchase of the Louisiana Territory by President Thomas Jefferson *(above)*.

1812–1814 War with Britain over free trade and sailors' rights.

1817–1825 The Erie Canal, built with immigrant labour, connects the Great Lakes and New York Harbour.

1820 The Missouri Compromise permits slavery in Missouri but bars it in the rest of the Louisiana Purchase, north of 36° 30'N.

1823 The Monroe Doctrine bans European interference in the Americas.

1845 Texas is annexed by Congress; the Mexican War results.

1848 Mexico cedes Texas, California, Arizona, Utah and Nevada to the United States as war ends. The California gold rush begins.

1855 Armed clashes occur in Kansas over the slavery issue.

1857 The Supreme Court's Dred Scott decision denies blacks constitutional rights on the ground they are not and cannot be citizens.

1859 Radical abolitionists seize the federal arsenal at Harpers Ferry under the leadership of John Brown. Brown is captured and hanged for treason.

1860 Abraham Lincoln *(above)* is elected to serve as President. South Carolina secedes from the Union over the issue of state's rights.

1861 The Confederate States of America are organized. Fort Sumter is bombarded *(below)* as the Civil War begins.

1862 Lincoln issues the Emancipation Proclamation. The Morrill Act provides land grants for state colleges.

1863 Victories of the North in the Gettysburg battle and the Vicksburg campaign are turning points of the War.

1865 The Civil War ends as Confederate General Robert E. Lee surrenders to General Ulysses S. Grant at Appomattox. Lincoln is assassinated.

1867 Alaska is purchased from Russia.

1868 The 14th Amendment is ratified, giving civil rights to blacks.

1869 The first transcontinental railway, built with immigrant Irish and Chinese labour, is completed.

1876 Alexander Graham Bell invents the telephone.

1879 Thomas A. Edison invents the incandescent light bulb.

1886 Twenty years' warfare with Western Indians comes to an end with Apache Chief Geronimo's surrender. The American Federation of Labour is formed and becomes the spearhead of the American labour movement.

1896 The Supreme Court upholds Southern segregation laws, "separate but equal" treatment of blacks.

1898 The Spanish–American War. Spain cedes the Philippines, Puerto Rico and Guam to the U.S., and guarantees Cuba's independence. Congress annexes the Hawaiian Islands.

1901 President William McKinley is assassinated; 43-year-old Theodore Roosevelt becomes the youngest United States President.

1903 The Wright brothers make the first successful powered flight, at Kitty Hawk, North Carolina.

1916 The Virgin Islands are purchased from Denmark.

1917–1918 U.S. forces fight in World War I *(above)*.

1920 The 18th Amendment goes into effect, prohibiting the sale of intoxicating liquors. Female suffrage is guaranteed by the 19th Amendment.

1924 Congress confers citizenship on American Indians.

1927 Charles A. Lindbergh makes the first non-stop solo flight across the Atlantic *(above)*.

1929 The U.S. stock market collapses, touching off a prolonged and worldwide economic depression.

1933 President Franklin D. Roosevelt *(above)* launches the "New Deal", which speeds the nation's economic recovery through social and economic reforms. Prohibition is repealed.

1941 The U.S. enters World War II after Japan bombs Pearl Harbor.

1942 Japanese–Americans are interned under the War Relocation Act.

1945 Germany surrenders. President Roosevelt dies; Harry S. Truman succeeds him in the White House. Atomic bombs are dropped on Hiroshima and Nagasaki; Japan surrenders.

1948 Congress passes the European Recovery Plan (the Marshall Plan).

1950–1953 The Korean War.

1954 The Supreme Court unanimously bars racial segregation in the public schools in its Brown vs. Board of Education decision.

1955 Martin Luther King Jr. leads a successful boycott of the segregated bus system in Montgomery, Alabama.

1959 Alaska and Hawaii become states.

1962 Lieutenant Colonel John Glenn becomes the first American to orbit the earth.

1963 President John F. Kennedy is assassinated in Dallas, Texas; Lyndon B. Johnson succeeds him.

1964 The Civil Rights Act goes into effect. U.S. planes begin combat missions over South Vietnam.

1967 Thurgood Marshall becomes the first black Supreme Court Justice.

1968 Martin Luther King Jr. is assassinated in Memphis, Tennessee. Robert Kennedy is shot in Los Angeles. The number of U.S. soldiers in Vietnam *(below)* climbs to half a million.

1969 First U.S. astronauts on the moon.

1972 The Watergate scandal begins.

1973 The Vietnam War ends with the signing of a four-power peace pact.

1974 President Richard Nixon resigns over Watergate; he is pardoned by President Gerald Ford.

1976 The nation's bicentennial.

1981 U.S. hostages are freed after more than a year in captivity in Iran. The space shuttle makes its maiden voyage. Sandra Day O'Connor becomes the first woman appointed to the Supreme Court.

1983 Sally K. Ride and Lieutenant Colonel Guion S. Bluford Jr. become America's first female and first black astronauts in space.

every now and then would be a healthy thing ("the tree of liberty," as he put it, needed periodically to be refreshed "by the blood of patriots and tyrants").

Hamilton was a self-made man. The illegitimate son of a West Indian merchant, he had gone to North America only in 1772, but by 1776, at the age of 26, he had already become chief aide-de-camp to George Washington, commander of the Revolutionary forces. Hamilton's political philosophy was tough and conservative. "All communities divide themselves into the few and the many," he said. The "few" were the "rich and well born". The rest were "the mass of the people". What government needed, above all, was stability, and the way to achieve it was to give the rich "a distinct, permanent share in the Government".

Hamilton and Jefferson both served in the Cabinet of George Washington, who was the nation's choice as first President. As Secretary of the Treasury, Hamilton carried out his policy of making the national government the friend of the rich. He set up a national bank to control lending and prevent the inflation that would have devalued the holdings of the well-to-do. He encouraged manufacturing through subsidies and protective tariffs. And he showed that the government meant business by using federal troops in 1794 to crush a small Pennsylvanian rebellion against an excise tax on liquor. (Outraged Pennsylvanian farmers simply wanted to distil their grain and sell it as good, tax-free Monongahela whiskey.)

Jefferson, meanwhile, left his post as Secretary of State to help organize a coalition that would fight Hamilton's policies. He failed in his attempt to become president as the candidate of the newly formed Democratic-Republican Party in 1796. The job went instead to John Adams, Hamilton's ally from Massachusetts. Adams, Hamilton and their Federalist Party proceeded to justify Jefferson's growing anxieties about the new government's despotic tendencies. Especially alarming was the passage, during what proved a short-lived crisis, of the Alien and Sedition Acts of 1798, which gave the president and the courts broad powers to expel foreigners and jail political critics.

Yet at that very point, when the young Constitution seemed in peril of collapsing, it proved equal to the crisis. In 1800 the Democratic-Republicans won the election, and the Federalists dutifully turned over the reins to Jefferson, who responded in his inaugural address with a wound-healing call for national unity. The "peaceful revolution" of 1800 was a landmark. It proved that bitterly opposed political factions could battle on, election by election, within the framework of the Constitution and without bloodshed.

Further tests were in the offing, caused largely by the wild surge of expansion that followed the conclusion of a second conflict with Britain, the War of 1812. Between then and 1860, by purchase, annexation and war, the U.S. added more than 5 million square kilometres of territory to its original 2.3 million. In that same half century the population swelled, largely due to immigration, from seven million to just over 30 million. By 1860 the original 13 states had increased to 33. At any time during the period there would have been truth in the remark made in 1817 by the South Carolina politician John C. Calhoun: "We are rapidly—I was about to say fearfully—growing."

Early in this explosive era, a new sort of rugged, highly individualistic American began to emerge, especially on the Western frontier, where settlers were unfettered by the traditions of the older Atlantic Seaboard society or even by very much government. The uninhibited Westerners demanded a greater voice for their region in the policies of the government. One way to get it was to enlarge the franchise, with every man having the vote. During the early decades of the century, a number of states—all of which had originally restricted voting rights to male property owners—passed universal manhood suffrage acts, although the emphasis was still on "man", and meant only "white man". The broadened electorate promptly provided the nation with a president who became the symbol of the age, Andrew Jackson.

He was markedly different from the scholar-politicians of the founding generation. Born to poverty in 1767 in the Carolinas, he taught himself law and moved to frontier Tennessee in the 1780s. There he became a prosperous community leader. When his neighbours elected him a judge, he expressed his judicial philosophy in simple terms: "Do what is right between parties. That is what the law means." He embodied what a later historian called the characteristic American qualities bred by the frontier experience: "Coarseness and strength combined with acuteness and inquisitiveness; restless, nervous energy; dominant individualism, working for good and for evil, and that buoyancy and exuberance which comes with freedom."

Jackson was a natural legend as a commander of frontier troops in the War of 1812: in the last battle, his sharpshooters virtually annihilated advancing British columns at New Orleans. In 1818, he again demon-

was much left to do. Inevitably, the country's most glaring violation of human rights, black slavery, became the focus of national attention. Anti-slavery movements had existed since colonial times, but they had proposed moderate solutions, such as gradual emancipation, with slaveholders being compensated for loss of property.

A new, immoderate tone was introduced to the debate by William Lloyd Garrison and his newspaper, *The Liberator*. An editor and printer from Massachusetts, he was self-righteous and in no way conciliatory. "I am in earnest," he wrote in *The Liberator's* first issue in 1831. "I will not equivocate—I will not excuse—I will not retreat a single inch; and I will be heard!" Slavery must be ended immediately, completely and without compensation. His war cry—and it would prove nothing less—was soon echoed by dozens of fellow abolitionists.

The abolitionists were right; the continuing forcible enslavement of four million black human beings was an intolerable wrong, especially in a nation supposedly dedicated to freedom and equality. But most Southerners did not see it that way. The South's entire economy, founded on cotton grown for export, was dependent on a reliable source of cheap labour. Further, many Southerners regarded slavery as a "positive good". Their slaves were better off, they said, than white mill hands shackled by economic necessity to the looms and lathes of Northern factories. Besides, the slaves benefited spiritually and morally by the Christian faith they learnt from their masters.

As this debate raged in pulpit and press, the growth of the nation inexorably brought the issue to a head. New states, most of which banned slavery,

strated his gift for military boldness by leading an invasion of Florida—Spanish territory at the time—without authorization from Washington.

There, Jackson rooted out a pair of British traders who were inciting the Seminole Indians to raid settlements in Georgia; he set up a court-martial and executed the two.

Frontier folk loved it and, to the horror of Eastern conservatives, helped to elect their hero President in 1828. Jackson proved a decisive chief executive, active on behalf of the people and especially those of his own Western region. His hostility to monopoly and privilege caused him to fight and destroy the Bank of the United States, which had controlled the money supply. With the bank's demise, the credit needed by farmers was easier to get. He opened land for settlement—unfortunately at the expense of the Indians. Above all, he embodied the idea that ordinary Americans, not just Eastern aristocrats, could run the country.

Although Jackson advanced the cause of true equality in America, there were formed and admitted to the Union as the people expanded westwards. By 1850, non-slave states outnumbered those that had slavery, and all the free states together had a total population 50 per cent greater than that of the slave states. The South's new minority status meant that the rest of the country possessed the legislative power, should it wish to use it, to outlaw slavery altogether, or to attack any other uniquely Southern institution.

This was the prospect particularly frightening to Southerners such as the brilliant but resolutely conservative John C. Calhoun. In his last speech as a senator, in 1850, he uttered a dire warning: unless the North agreed to changes to restore the "equilibrium" between the two sections, it would be evident that the North's objects were "power and aggrandizement". The South would then have no choices but "submission or resistance".

Calhoun wanted nothing less than federal guarantees that slavery would never be outlawed, not only in the states, but also in the still sparsely settled Western territories, where the American future lay. That, in its turn, was intolerable to Northern moderates like Abraham Lincoln, a poor-born, self-taught lawyer who struggled to reconcile his frank hatred of slavery with his profound respect for the Constitution, which protected slavery in those states that wanted it. Slavery, said Lincoln, denied the basic promise of the Declaration of Independence, "that in due time the weights would be lifted from the shoulders of all men and that all should have an equal chance".

In the proposals of the new Republican party, founded in 1854, Lincoln found a middle ground that he hoped would avoid war. Slavery could stay in the states that already had it, where it would probably die as the progressive spirit of the age gradually caught up with the South. But it must not be allowed in the Western territories, which should be consecrated to "free labour". This compromise was wholly unacceptable to Calhoun's successors in the South's leadership. The position of the two sections was irreconcilable.

Lincoln's election to the presidency in 1860 made the South realize it was futile to remain in the Union. Eleven Southern states seceded and formed the Confederate States of America. The North took up arms rather than see the Union destroyed. Lincoln's often-quoted words, delivered in Gettysburg, Pennsylvania, in 1863 made clear that the Civil War, to Northerners at least, was not a mere sectional struggle but a momentous test of whether a nation "conceived in Liberty, and dedicated to the proposition that all men are created equal" could "long endure".

Paradox abounded. Slavery was at the root of the War, but the North did

Striking a warlike pose, a Confederate volunteer, Private William B. Todd of the 9th Virginia Cavalry, holds his pistol at the ready in an old ambrotype. The Civil War saw ghastly slaughter; one out of every four men who served perished.

not begin combat with any avowed intention of ending slavery. Southerners insisted that their basic cause was not preservation of slavery but simply self-determination—the cause of the colonies in 1776. In the end, the necessities of war destroyed what the South called its "peculiar institution". Lincoln freed the slaves by proclamation in 1863, partly because Northern public opinion demanded it, partly to help recruit blacks into the Union armies and partly to convince Britain and other European countries, which had been inclined to aid the South, that the North was fighting a "moral cause".

By the time the bloody conflict ended, in 1865, the North was in a mood of mingled idealism and vengefulness. The states ratified not only the 13th Amendment to the Constitution, abolishing slavery everywhere, but also the 14th and 15th, conferring citizenship and suffrage on all male Americans regardless of race—with the single, glaring exception of Indians, who had to wait until 1924.

The latter two amendments proved hard to enforce. After 11 years of occupation of the beaten South, federal troops were withdrawn as the North turned back to their business as usual. Blacks, left to the untender mercies of the white Southern majority, were quickly relegated to a distinctly inferior status, for the most part without votes, without equal rights and without the law's protection of their property or even their lives.

Still, the War had been a victory for the ideal (if not the fact) of equality and established that the nation could and would "long endure". Both sides had resorted to fighting in the name of freedom. But ironically one of the freedoms that the Confederates wanted was the

2

freedom to deny freedom to others. Nothing more tragically illustrated the difficulty of reconciling different American notions of individual liberty and social good than the 500,000 lives lost in the sectional struggle.

The end of the war liberated new whirlwinds of energy. Pioneer farmers poured into the West. Using new machines, they produced grain and livestock that Western cities such as Minneapolis, Kansas City, St. Louis and Chicago transformed into enough flour and canned meat to feed millions. Roaring blast furnaces in Pennsylvania poured out rivers of molten iron and steel. Everywhere Americans heard the clang and hum of machines that mass-produced typewriters, trams, shoes and carpets, furniture, clothing and other consumer goods.

In this increasingly industrialized society, which numbered 75 million people by 1900, the Constitution framed for an agrarian republic of four million was strained once again. The men who controlled the mechanical marvels boasted that their success was evidence of what exceptional individuals could achieve, given enough freedom. These pre-eminent beneficiaries of the *laissez-faire* economy included Cornelius Vanderbilt, who went from illiterate ferryboatman to railway mogul in a lifetime of hard bargaining and ruining his competitors; and John D. Rockefeller, a pious but ruthless bookkeeper who amassed oil wells, and formed the Standard Oil Company, the colossus of the petroleum industry.

Such men frequently did not do corporate contest with their competition. Instead they formed alliances, or they bought out their competitors, creating combinations called "trusts" that had total control of whole industries. These individuals wielded prodigious power—power to rig prices, pay workers the lowest possible wages or even throw entire communities out of work. They bought newspapers to propagate their opinions and shamelessly bribed judges and legislators. The gulf between them and those who worked for them—coal miners crushed or gassed in unsafe mines, children dragging themselves through the drab alleys of company towns to work 12-hour days—grew wider and wider.

Liberty had led to a gross inequality, aptly described in the 1892 platform of the People's Party, a short-lived political organization of wheat and cotton farmers radicalized by hard times and falling prices. "From the same prolific womb of governmental injustice," they said, "we breed the two great classes of tramps and millionaires."

The pendulum of democratic thinking inevitably swung back towards asserting society's right to intervene on behalf of the powerless. Some of the citizens pressed their case by independent organization, without waiting for government to stir itself to redress the balance. Workers who joined the growing labour movement during the late 19th century, in fact, often had to fight government as well as employers, because laws that protected the freedom of entrepreneurs to make money denied working people their freedom to organize unions and to strike.

The chief political impetus for reform came from what was called the Progressive movement. The progressives were men and women who were born or raised after the Civil War and who carried forward the humanitarian and evangelistic impulses of the abolitionists and other early crusaders into the industrial age. Through their zest, the state and city statute books were soon peppered with new laws (bitterly

AN AMERICAN TRAGEDY

The opening of the West, a great American saga, had its dark side. It drove the Indians from their land, even in areas set aside by treaty as refuges. The Treaty of Laramie typified the process of dispossession. Signed (*far right*) by Red Cloud and his fellow chiefs in 1868, it gave the Sioux and other tribes about half of present-day South Dakota. But the pact, like so many others, was not kept. The lure of gold attracted white miners into the refuge's Black Hills, which the Sioux held sacred. Outraged Indians attacked, and war ensued. Eventually the entire preserve was usurped. In 1871 Congress scrapped all the treaties and began to establish the much-reduced Indian reservations that exist today.

Chief Red Cloud sits for a photograph in 1880.

opposed by the big corporations) requiring health and safety inspections of factories, compensation for job-related injuries or deaths, and limits on the hours that women and children could work. Slowly the country edged towards control of industrial evils.

But the movement needed a major champion if it was to achieve its ends at the federal level. Progressivism found its national leader in Theodore Roosevelt. A man of enormous energy and self-confidence, Roosevelt came from New York's old mercantile aristocracy. Overcoming weak eyes and childhood asthma, he turned himself into a rugged physical specimen who was forever hiking, hunting, riding, boxing and playing tennis. Before he became Vice President at the age of 42, in 1901, Roosevelt had been New York City Police Commissioner, Assistant Secretary of the Navy, commander of a cavalry regiment in the Spanish–American War and New York Governor.

When the assassination of President William McKinley put Roosevelt in the White House, he turned his talent for zestful action to a crusade against concentrated corporate wealth. The only weapon available to him was a blunt instrument, the Sherman Anti-Trust Act of 1890. It declared "combinations in restraint of trade" to be illegal, but it had been rarely enforced—except against labour unions. Roosevelt ordered the Department of Justice to employ the Act by initiating anti-trust suits. The Department did so, dismembering a railway combine engineered by J. P. Morgan, E. H. Harriman and James J. Hill, three of America's most powerful millionaires.

Roosevelt then turned to giving organized labour a boost. He settled a major coal strike by forcing the mine owners to sit down with a union representative in Washington, D.C., thus officially recognizing labour's right to negotiate. He crusaded for other reforms. From what he called the "bully pulpit" of the White House, he lent his weight to journalistic exposés of tainted meat and poisonous patent medicines, and secured passage of the Pure Food and Drug Act. He fought diligently for land conservation, protecting millions of wilderness hectares from commercial exploitation.

But beneath the turbulence of his reforms, Roosevelt steered a basically moderate course. He might denounce "the representatives of predatory wealth" as guilty of "all forms of iniquity from the oppression of wage workers to defrauding the public", but he was selective about what trusts he tried to bust. He saw some corporations as inevitable and a tolerable format for non-monopolistic industries.

His aim was to save the soul of the nation only from the extremes of wealth

Chiefs meet government delegates, mostly Army officers, at Fort Laramie, Wyoming, to sign a short-lived territorial treaty.

65

and poverty, promising Americans what he called a "Square Deal".

Roosevelt left the White House in 1909 after two terms as President, but when Conservatives gained control of the Republican Party in 1912 he ran again under the banner of a new, third party: the Progressives. The party platform called for a number of reformist measures, including federal regulation of corporations, the prohibition of child labour, unemployment insurance for workers and national standards for industrial health and safety.

Roosevelt lost the election to Woodrow Wilson, the Democratic candidate. But some of the principles of the Progressive Party were adopted by Wilson, himself a reform-minded exemplar of progressive attitudes. Just as the anti-federalists had got 10 amendments into the U.S. Constitution and the abolitionists three, the Progress-

ives succeeded in adding three between 1913 and 1920. The 16th created the income tax, which could (and later did) become an instrument for the re-allocation of wealth through heavier taxes on higher incomes. The 17th provided for the direct election of senators (formerly chosen by their state legislatures). The 19th gave votes to women, thanks largely to female leadership in the Progressive Party. (The 18th, repealed after 14 years, prohibited the manufacture or sale of alcoholic beverages.)

World War I and the economic prosperity that followed in the Roaring Twenties temporarily sidetracked the impulse towards reform. But in the early 1930s, a worldwide depression savaged the American economy. By 1932, one quarter of the work force was on the streets and half the country's productive machinery was idle. Capitalism seemed to be on its last legs and

America was swept by alarmist talk of revolutions. The country needed a fresh dose of ideas for reviving the general welfare. It got them from Franklin Delano Roosevelt.

This Roosevelt, known by the press as F.D.R., was only a distant cousin of the former President, but he shared much of the same Rooseveltian energy and political skill. On taking office in 1933 he captured the faith of most Americans with his bold words and bold deeds. "The only thing we have to fear," he told them, "is fear itself," and he began pushing through Congress a radical collection of programmes that he termed a "New Deal".

Some of Roosevelt's programmes were designed primarily as emergency measures to patch up a badly wounded economy. The unemployed were put to work on a multitude of government-financed public projects. They built

Their eyes revealing more defeat than hope, a weary family sets off from Oklahoma in 1939 in quest of a better life. During the Depression, thousands of families left the Dust Bowl, a region of prairie farmland ruined by overuse and erosion.

courthouses, post offices, bridges, dams, airports and thousands of kilometres of roads. By reforestation and flood control, they reclaimed millions of hectares of soil from erosion and devastation. The New Deal was literally stamped on the American landscape.

Other programmes reflected long-term reform principles. Taken as a whole, the New Deal amounted to a peaceful revolution that, for all the enmity it earned from conservative businessmen, preserved and strengthened the private-enterprise system while also bringing the federal government into direct and almost daily contact with the citizenry. A New Deal agency, the Securities and Exchange Commission, still guards investors against fraud in the stock and bond markets. The National Labour Relations Board (set up in 1935) still protects the right to collective bargaining. Every Social Security payment to the elderly and disabled is the result of an act passed under Roosevelt's leadership in 1935.

Both the Square Deal and the New Deal were variations on the theme of promoting the well-being of the people as a whole. Subsequent presidents were to play the tune again under various titles, from the end of World War II into the 1960s. Harry Truman had his Fair Deal, John Kennedy his New Frontier, and Lyndon Johnson his Great Society. But the 1960s were marked by another sort of ferment that recalled those strenuous searches for individual liberty, coupled somehow with equality, that had characterized earlier periods of American history.

It was leftover business from the Civil War, in fact, that was largely responsible for the new period of unrest. In 1954, the Supreme Court ruled that the segregation of black children in their own separate public schools was un-Constitutional. That long-deferred decision provoked strong resistance among whites in Southern communities, but it inspired a new generation of black men and women to a new attack on the barriers that surrounded them.

They found non-violent but effective ways of dramatizing their demands—the sit-in, the boycott, the mass march, the demonstration—under the leadership of a young black clergyman, Martin Luther King Jr., whose eloquence touched the national conscience. His work secured the passage of strong federal civil rights and voting rights acts in 1964 and 1965, and won him a Nobel Peace Prize in 1964. It also, in 1968, brought an assassin's bullet.

Roger Williams, seeking separation of church and state in Massachusetts in the 1630s, and Martin Luther King Jr., struggling for equal rights for all in the 1960s, were linked by a chain of American traditions: the belief that government exists mainly for the purpose of protecting individual rights. The black revolt proved contagious. Women, Native Americans, Hispanics, homosexuals and other groups previously denied admission to the mainstream of American life organized themselves to demand a fair share of power. Equality, they said, was for everybody.

The success of these several movements renewed in many Americans a confidence in their ability to influence their nation's course. They challenged the very authority of their elected government at every unpopular turn. With the help of a Congress newly responsive to the people's will, they brought an end to a disliked and lengthy war in Vietnam, persuaded one President (Lyndon Johnson) not to run for re-election and compelled another (Richard Nixon) to resign before completing his term of office.

As the protest movements mounted in volume, they provoked an inevitable backlash. Some of the critics questioned the wisdom of placing congressional constraints on the president's authority to use military force or secret operations in pursuit of the country's aims abroad. Others challenged domestic programmes created to afford opportunities to long-frustrated minorities. Should the government, they asked, offer special help to one group of citizens, even for the worthiest motives, if it was at the expense of others?

Moreover, each new civil rights guarantee logically required new enforcement machinery, with the result that the weight of government seemed to some to be growing oppressively heavy. This produced its own backlash against all the difficult years of reform and the bureaucracy that accompanied it. Followers of the Progressive gospel began to find the going hard.

But when reform was challenged, it was almost always challenged in democratic terms. Many of the debates of the early 1980s—on the limits of governmental powers, on a woman's right to an abortion, on prayer in schools—came down in the end to the same enduring root questions. What can government do to help all Americans achieve the blessings of liberty? And what must it refrain from doing to make sure that each person enjoys as fully as possible both liberty and the right to pursue happiness?

The language that rings out from the television sets and in print is contemporary, but the issues at the heart of the discussions would not be unfamiliar to John Winthrop, Thomas Jefferson, John Calhoun or Abraham Lincoln.

Henry G. Wilks	Ricanthony R. Ashley	Dino D. Dutcher	Lisa K. Wallace
Polish	Jamaican	Italian	American Indian
German	Spanish	English	English
Scottish	American Indian	Irish	German
American Indian	French		Irish
Irish	English		
English	African		

CHILDREN OF THE MELTING POT

Americans are proud of their varied ancestries. Just how diverse these can be is suggested by the lineage of the members of a typical squad of cadets *(above)* at the United States Military Academy at West Point, New York. The family trees of these nine men and women show a total of 14 ethnic strains, ranging from English, German and Irish to African and American Indian.

Certain ethnic strains are stronger than others in the population of the U.S. as a whole. According to the 1980 census, some 50 million Americans, about one fourth of the 1980 U.S. population, are of English descent—more

Leslie A. Lewis
French
Welsh
German
Irish

Kevin A. Moore
Icelandic
Scottish
Irish

Jamie L. McCloud
African
American Indian

William F. Willoughby
German
English
Scottish
Irish

John T. Snider
Japanese
German
Irish

people than live in England and Wales today. Another 49 million Americans identify themselves as descendants of German immigrants, a number equal to almost two thirds of the total population of East and West Germany. Americans of Irish descent, a total of 40 million,

outnumber by 12 to 1 the population of the Irish Republic.

The peak period of immigration for Europeans was the six decades from 1871 to 1930, when 30,385,000 men, women and children arrived on America's shores; from 1901 to 1910, almost nine million people were admitted. In the later

decades, immigration has slowed down, but has by no means come to a halt. From 1941 to 1979, there were 10.8 million new arrivals, who enriched the nation's ethnic mix further. More than 215,000 Vietnamese now consider the United States their homes, as do 120,000 Iranians and 90,000 Haitians.

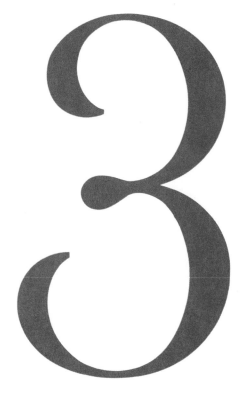

At the first and largest solar electrical generating plant in the U.S., in the Californian desert, more than 1,800 sun-tracking mirrors, or heliostats, surround the 91-metre-high tower. Each heliostat *(inset)* beams reflected sunlight at the boiler on the tower to produce steam and drive a turbine.

AN ECONOMY
OF ABUNDANCE

In 1807, a Connecticut clockmaker by the name of Eli Terry contracted to make the parts and assemble the movements for 4,000 grandfather clocks at the unheard-of low price of four dollars apiece. The buyer would construct the clock cases and market the finished product. Many of Terry's fellow clockmakers thought he was out of his mind. Making a clock was an intricate process involving such traditional hand tools as hammer, saw, file and drill. Even with the help of an apprentice or two, a master craftsman could produce only about 20 clocks a year, each of them selling for about $50.

Terry had been in the business for 15 years; he knew that traditional methods would not allow him to turn out 400 clocks, let alone 4,000, in the three years allotted him. But he had a bold plan. He intended to use machines to shape each component of the clockworks to a standard pattern and size. Then these interchangeable parts could be quickly assembled into complete movements. The idea was not new: a fellow Connecticut entrepreneur, Eli Whitney, was attempting to use a similar system to produce 10,000 muskets for the U.S. government. But Terry was the first to apply the notion to a consumer product.

With the help of two apprentices, Terry converted an old gristmill. By a system of shafts and belts, he harnessed the mill's water wheel to the lathes, saws and other tools that would turn out the interchangeable clock parts. He went into production, and by the final year of the contract, he and his apprentices could manufacture more clock movements in a day than a comparable work force could make by hand in a year. His total of 3,000 movements for that year fulfilled the contract. For perhaps the first time in history, true mass production of a household mechanical device had been achieved.

Even with mass production, however, the elaborate grandfather clock was still beyond the means of most Americans. So Terry designed a new clock that was only 50 centimetres high—small enough to stand on a shelf. By mass production and effective marketing, he was able to sell this model directly to customers for only $15, a price that made it possible for the average American to own a clock.

The techniques of mass production pioneered in the U.S. by Eli Terry and others formed the foundation for what later became known as the "American system" for manufacturing. The concept of mechanized, large-scale production quickly spread beyond the walls of the factory, transforming work in such other sectors of the American economy as mining and, above all, agriculture. Terry, one historian has written, was "the last of the craftsmen and the first of the industrialists".

The United States in the early 19th century was ripe for such innovation. The land was brimming with natural

71

3

resources from which things could be made in great quantity; Terry, for example, made his clock movements from wood instead of brass because timber was abundant and cheap. Moreover, there was a market for goods in quantity. The nation was open to trade, and its commerce was unhindered by the tariff barriers that divided and hobbled the European economy.

And the American people hankered after a better life. Terry knew instinctively that not just the wealthy but any farm family might be induced to buy a clock if it was inexpensive enough. As American historian David Potter has observed, "European radical thought is prone to demand that the man of property be stripped of his carriage and his fine clothes. But American radical thought is likely to insist, instead, that the ordinary man is entitled to mass-produced copies, indistinguishable from the originals."

Producing goods in quantity was only the beginning. The same forces led inevitably to what became another dominant feature of the U.S. economy, the provision of services en masse. At first, services—work that in itself does not produce a commodity—centred upon transporting the goods and selling them. Later, as industry became highly efficient, the proportion of the work force needed to produce goods declined: an increasing number went into education, health care, government, communications, and restaurant and hotel management, helping to fulfil ever-rising American expectations of the good life.

By the 1980s, in fact, the provision of services had long since displaced the production of goods as the principal economic activity in the United States, employing nearly 70 per cent of the 100-million-member working labour force. In 1982, the total output of goods and services—the country's gross national product, or GNP—amounted to a staggering $3.1 trillion, or roughly one fifth of all the goods and services produced in the world.

The result is a standard of living rivalled by few other nations. In the early 1980s, the U.S. per capita income was $11,000, one of the highest among industrialized countries. By 1980, 77 per cent of all U.S. households had a washing machine, 43 per cent a dishwasher, 45 per cent a freezer, and 98 per cent had telephone service.

Some of America's prosperity, of course, is attributable to two world wars that dislocated other countries' economies while actually spurring growth in the U.S. But wartime booms cannot account for all or even most of the extraordinary gains in productivity over the years. From 1909 to 1982, the output per paid worker-hour in U.S. factories increased four and a half times. Such gains must be credited not only to the invention and installation of better machines, but also to advances in the training of both workers and managers. Down through the years America has spawned or lured from abroad thousands of resourceful industrial pioneers who—driven by their ambition for wealth or power, or by the plain thrill of doing something better than anyone had ever done it before—have put the nation at the forefront of technological progress.

The list of the nation's business geniuses includes men like Andrew Carnegie, a Scottish immigrant who became a steelmaker in 1872. The steel industry at that time was a shambles of small companies—each specializing in one stage of production, from ore

FINANCIAL HEART OF THE FARM BELT

The United States is a nation of investors: an estimated one out of every five Americans owns stock. For the intrepid, there are riskier forms of investment, such as trading in commodities—grain, meat, precious metals and dozens of other products. In a typical commodities transaction, investors buy and sell "futures"—contracts to deliver or take delivery of large amounts of goods at a later date and at the price fixed in the contracts.

The risk is great because commodity prices can fluctuate wildly; an unexpected cancellation in a large export sale can send wheat prices plummeting, hurting investors who bought contracts at higher prices. Futures can also soar or drop from minute to minute in response to rumours and investors' hopes and fears concerning supply and demand. Speculators can make a million dollars in a week of buying and selling futures. Millionaires have lost fortunes just as swiftly.

The nation's most active commodities exchange is the Chicago Board of Trade *(right)*, which also deals in financial instruments such as Treasury bonds. It was founded in 1848 by 82 Chicago merchants to provide a central trading facility for the Midwest's grain farmers. Establishing prices for crops not yet harvested (or even planted) led to the trade in futures. Today the Board of Trade is housed in a huge building in central Chicago. It has more than 3,000 members, some of them independent speculators and some traders who act for brokerage houses and wear coloured jackets to indicate the firms they represent.

Life in the stepped-down octagonal "pits" where individual commodities are traded is grimly serious. "It's ferocious," one trader has said; "it's man against man." Another trader declared: "There are no friends in the pit. You do not take prisoners in here."

As a tally board records prices *(top left)*, traders jam one of the floors of Chicago's Board of Trade.

A janitor cleans up the debris after a trading session in one of the Board's pits *(above)*. On the right, soy-bean traders with membership badges use hand signals to execute orders; the man with four fingers extended and palm outward is selling four soy-bean contracts, or 70,000 hectolitres.

3

smelting to making finished goods—and middlemen who bought and resold the partially processed metal at every stage. Worse, the manufacturers did not know their running costs; they discovered whether they had made a profit or loss only at the end of the year, when their books were balanced.

Carnegie cut out the middlemen by combining all steps of production in his company. By careful measurement of materials, fuel use, man-hours and equipment life, he determined his true running costs—applying, in short, what modern business calls cost accounting. And he drove those costs down by reinvesting his profits in new machines whenever he found any that could make a product faster or with less

manpower. He once tore down a rolling mill only three months old when he learnt of a new design that would make production cheaper.

Over a span of 20 years, Carnegie cut the cost of making steel by almost four fifths. By 1900 his company was producing almost as much as the entire British steel industry, and his profits were 20 times as great as they had been only 12 years earlier.

American industrialists of the 20th century added their own innovations to the accomplishments of men like Terry and Carnegie. This was especially true of leaders in the car industry, which in time became the country's biggest. In 1901 one of the early carmakers, Ransom Eli Olds, fused the system of using

interchangeable parts with an idea from the meat-packing business, where beef travelled on overhead trolleys as it was processed. The result was the very symbol of modern mass production: the car assembly line. Cars under construction moved past the line of workers, each of whom added a part or parts. In 1904, Olds produced 4,000 of his Oldsmobiles, a phenomenal number for the era.

Four years later, Henry Ford improved on Olds's system by breaking down the assembly process into ever-smaller and ever-simpler tasks, each of which was handled by one person and with as few motions as possible. Off the end of the line rolled the first Ford Model T, the car that put America on

wheels and touched off the explosive growth of the U.S. car industry. The first Model T took 12 hours and 28 minutes to assemble; by 1914, Ford had cut the time down to 93 minutes. Thanks to improved production methods, the retail price of a Model T dropped 49 per cent over a five-year period, putting the car within the financial reach of the average American family. Henry Ford's devotion to cost-cutting led him to avoid all frills; he used to say that the customer could have a Model T in any colour he or she wanted, "so long as it is black".

Ford's technical achievements in the car industry enabled him to dominate the marketplace until the 1920s, when a genius of a different stripe, Alfred P. Sloan Jr., applied his own brilliant insights to a company called General Motors, or GM.

General Motors was then run by William C. Durant, a wheeler-dealer who made crucial decisions by intuition as he juggled the receivers of the 10 continually ringing telephones on his desk. Sloan, a vice president of the company, despaired over Durant's haphazard management, which was bringing GM close to ruin.

Sloan proposed a restructuring of GM that would disperse authority and ensure that decisions were made only after careful consideration of the facts. Durant took no notice, and Sloan was about to resign, when the Du Pont Company, a giant munitions manufacturer and one of the firm's major stockholders, became alarmed about GM's shaky condition. It forced Durant to resign and later installed Sloan as chief executive officer.

Sloan immediately began delegating authority to the heads of GM's various divisions while building a strong cen-

tral staff to set policy and make market forecasts. He preached a new concept of profitability: the amount of money a company earns is less important than the ratio of that profit to the invested capital. This notion of "return on investment" became gospel to American business. Sloan also devised perhaps the most successful commercial sales gimmick in history; he initiated the practice of visibly altering car models every year, unashamedly admitting that he wanted "to make you dissatisfied with your current car so you will buy a new one".

Good managers like Sloan knew the value of creative talent, and American industry—as well as the U.S. government—has for most of the 20th century employed ideas people and devoted huge sums of money to research and development. Out of such research has come a dazzling list of products, including plastics, nylon and polyester—synthetics that revolutionized the packaging and clothing industries and today find thousands of applications around the world.

Occasionally a new product will come along that consumers never knew they needed until its sudden appearance in the marketplace. A case in point is the instant camera. It was invented by Edwin Land, a Harvard University dropout who in his brief but successful career obtained more than 500 patents, an achievement second only to that of the most prolific of American inventors, Thomas Edison.

Since 1888, when George Eastman introduced his inexpensive Kodak box camera and made everyone a photographer ("you press the button, we do the rest"), few Americans had felt any great need for film that could be developed on the spot. Then one day in

1943, Edwin Land's three-year-old daughter, Jennifer, asked why she could not see immediately the photograph that he had just snapped of her.

Why not, indeed? Land had already demonstrated his inventive genius, devising a sheet of polarized plastic that could be used in sun glasses and camera filters to cut down on glare. Within an hour of Jennifer's question, Land had worked out in his head the design of a camera that would in effect compress in its innards the apparatus of an entire darkroom. His instant camera, which was five years in the making, is now the basis of a two-billion-dollar-a-year industry that serves such markets as medicine and electronics as well as amateur photography.

There are few more dramatic examples of the benefits of research than the stunning breakthroughs in electronics. American predominance in this field dates back to 1947 and the development of the transistor by scientists working at the Bell Telephone Laboratories, the world's largest industrial research organization.

The transistor could control and amplify electric signals much faster and more efficiently than the old bulky vacuum tubes that had been widely used since the early 1920s. Over the next three decades, such devices were made smaller and speedier. By the 1980s, thousands of microscopic transistors were being routinely inscribed on individual flecks of silicon no bigger than the thumb of a newborn baby. Known as integrated circuits—or chips—these slivers of silicon can store tens of thousands of bits of information. Other chips, called microprocessors, contain both the memory and the logic functions of a complete computer. At a cost of $25, one microprocessor can do

Industrial robots send out crackling sparks as they weld new cars in a Delaware assembly plant. The robots cost $100,000 each, but 30 of them can weld 100 cars an hour, a 60 per cent improvement on the output of the same number of human workers.

3

the work of a computer that as recently as 1960 sold for $100,000.

Reduced production costs made the computer-based "high technology" economical not only for large businesses but for thousands of small firms and—through relatively low-priced personal computers—millions of households. Thus, when the old "smokestack" industries such as steel and car production were declining because of foreign competition and other forces, a mass market for high-tech goods and services was created. The new market spurred enormous industrial growth in places such as Boston and the area south of San Francisco known as Silicon Valley. For example, California's Intel Corporation, which developed the first microprocessor in 1971, mushroomed from 42 employees in 1968 to 20,000 in 1983.

That is the way most Americans feel their economy should function—as a marketplace where competition for the consumer's dollars encourages innovation, and entrepreneurs with good new ideas can become millionaires almost overnight. Such a picture of the U.S. economic system, however, is not complete. Although the United States probably comes closer than any other Western country except West Germany to having a pure free-enterprise economy, it is still true that government—at the federal, state and local levels—plays a large role in that economy. Government is the biggest spender, dispensing 28 per cent of the gross national product and absorbing, in the form of taxes, 20 per cent of that product to pay for its operations.

The government's effects on the economy are myriad and all-pervasive. Since the 1950s, the federal government has tried to reduce fluctuations in

the business cycle by the use of fiscal policy (taxation and government spending) and monetary policy (controlling the money supply via the quasi-independent Federal Reserve System, which functions much like the central banks of Europe).

During business recessions, the government has pumped demand into the flagging economy by spending more or taxing less—or both—thus expanding its budget deficit. During periods of economic growth, it has attempted to curb its deficit. But in the quarter century following 1957, the federal government balanced its annual budget only twice. Its tendency to create ever-larger deficits has often been blamed for driving up interest rates and pushing private borrowers—companies seeking money for expansion, or individuals who want loans for houses or cars—out of the credit markets.

In recent years, monetary policy has played an increasingly prominent role

in government attempts to stabilize the economy. While the government has achieved some success in levelling out the boom-and-bust cycles of earlier eras, its policies have not eliminated the pattern of accelerating inflation alternating with painful recession. Many people suspect the government has often compounded the problems.

Fiscal and monetary policies are not the only areas in which government is involved in the American economy. Government regulates business to ensure competition, and to protect the interests of workers and consumers. Almost all Americans have some pet gripe about government interference with their economic freedom. But just about all also have reason to be thankful for the government's involvement in the economy (although they rarely say so out loud) or to ask for even more involvement. Magazine and book publishers cherish their favourable postal rates. Steelworkers and car manufacturers ask for tighter import controls to protect them from foreign competition. Transport firms and oil companies resist higher taxes while pleading for more of the tax-supported motorways that help to make them prosperous.

The sector of the American economy in which government has been most directly involved—with results both good and bad—is agriculture. American farmers are the most productive the world has ever known. In 1850, one U.S. farm worker produced enough food and fibre for four persons; by 1980 one worker produced enough for 78. Though they constitute only about 3 per cent of the U.S. labour force, 3.7 million farm workers feed and help clothe the entire nation and much of the rest of the world. U.S. farmers produce 64 per cent of the world's soy beans, 46 per cent of its corn, 21 per cent of its meat and 17 per cent of its wheat. So much is left over after taking care of America's own substantial appetites that nearly one third of the annual farm production is exported.

This astonishing success stems in part from American agriculture's unrivalled natural blessings: a favourable climate and vast stretches of fertile soil. But it also has to do with government's long-standing involvement with agriculture. The government gave away land to settlers. It established agricultural colleges and a network of county agents to develop more efficient ways of nurturing crops and animals and to teach these new ways to farmers. It promoted the electrification of farms and subsidized extensive irrigation projects (about one fourth the total value of U.S. farm production comes from irrigated land). And for decades it has provided low-interest loans to farmers.

Government and private research has led to quantum leaps in the science of farming: new, higher-yielding hybrid plants and animals; supercharged fertilizers; chemicals that clear fields of weeds and insects; artificial-insemination techniques and embryo transplants that improve livestock.

Today, U.S. agriculture is a high-tech industry where productivity has grown much more rapidly than in any other sector of the economy. In contrast to the romantic image of man and the earth, the American farmer is likely to spend less time with his hands in the soil than the average suburban gardener. He may plan his crops with the aid of a home computer, plant his fields on a huge, 300-horsepower tractor, and irrigate them with a turbine-powered sprinkler that can water about 54 hectares at once. Today, tractors on U.S. farms outnumber workers.

Ironically, government intervention to aid agriculture has created a serious problem: federal price-support programmes have led to huge surpluses.

Haitian workers plant celery seedlings in the deep, black soil of the Glades, 2,285 square kilometres of rich alluvial land created when part of Florida's swampy Everglades was drained. As an almost year-round supplier of vegetables, the area is known as the "winter salad bowl".

3

Had agriculture been left to free-market forces, constantly increasing farm production would have resulted in such low prices that many American farmers would have gone broke. Those who survived could then have demanded higher prices for their crops. That would have hurt the food-buying American consumer—until the higher prices again inspired farmers to produce yet more, driving prices down again and condemning more farmers to financial ruin.

Since 1933, the federal government has tried to stabilize prices at a fair level for farmers by introducing a variety of programmes. These have included stepping in to buy up surpluses when prices dropped too low, paying farmers subsidies to take land out of production, selling surpluses abroad or giving them away to Third World countries, and issuing food stamps, with which America's poor could purchase food they could not otherwise afford.

The results have been mixed. The United States can give away only a limited amount of food abroad or at home without harming the agricultural economy of another nation and its own as well. Yet the notion of paying farmers to refrain from producing food when a large proportion of the world's population, including some Americans, go to bed hungry each night seems immoral to many people.

Some farmers complain that the government has not gone far enough to support agricultural prices and help them stay in business. But at least the federal programmes seem to have slowed the reduction in the number of farmers as productivity increased.

The government's programmes certainly did not stop that reduction. In 1950, 15.3 per cent of Americans lived

Weed-covered dykes trace sinuous patterns through a paddy field in California's Sacramento Valley. Most of the 1,375 square kilometres of California that are devoted to rice cultivation are sown by aeroplane.

3

on farms; by 1981, the figure had shrunk to just 2.5 per cent. During that period the average farm more than doubled in size, to about 180 hectares, and this enabled it to make efficient use of technology. The number of farms, meanwhile, declined by more than half, from 5.6 million to 2.3 million.

Even this statistic fails to convey the full extent of the changes down on the farm. The true working farms are now vastly outnumbered by weekend hobby farms for the well-to-do, or part-time operations that supplement wages earned from jobs in town. Only about 20 per cent of all farms have annual sales of $40,000 or more, yet they are responsible for nearly 80 per cent of U.S. agricultural production.

Farms fall into two basic categories by ownership: family farms and corporate farms. Despite repeated predictions of the demise of family-owned farms, they still account for nearly 90 per cent of America's agricultural land and 82 per cent of sales. While some farmers continue to diversify, producing grain, a variety of livestock and vegetables *(pages 84–91)*, most find greater profits in specialization. They produce only cattle or chickens or pigs or grain, and often concentrate on one stage of the production of their speciality, such as fattening pigs.

Farms like these form the base of the multibillion-dollar-a-year structure of enterprises collectively known as agribusiness. The interest a farmer pays on loans supports the local bank; the trac-

tors he buys help to sustain the dealer and the manufacturer; the fattened pigs he takes to market provide business for the meat-packer as well as the supermarket. Agribusiness employs more than 23 million people, or 22 per cent of America's labour force, and has fostered a new breed of entrepreneur.

Abraham Neufeld, who owns a farm in central Kansas, goes one step further than the specialist—he does not even farm his land. He rents out his 80 hectares to a neighbour and earns his own living from a fleet of six combine harvesters. Each of these machines—8 metres long and 4 metres wide—can cut and thresh 1,000 hectolitres of wheat a day. Every May, Neufeld, his family and a small group of hired hands begin a four-month pilgrimage. They move from Oklahoma north to the Canadian border, contracting their harvesting service to farmers who find it more profitable to hire someone like Neufeld than to own such expensive machinery themselves.

Each harvester has a soundproofed, air-conditioned cab with a stereo to entertain the driver and a computer to monitor the machine's operation and warn him if anything goes wrong. The Neufelds harvest about 8,000 hectares of wheat every summer, then switch attachments on the machines and set off to cut many hectares more of later-maturing corn.

Where the nature of the agricultural product lends itself to the economies of truly large-scale production, corporate farms have become increasingly dominant. In the production of cane sugar and cotton, for example, the necessary investments in land and technology are out of reach for most family farmers.

Corporations also have made inroads into the raising of other crops. In California's San Joaquin Valley, Tejon Agricultural Partners (TAP) uses the latest in technology on 5,000 hectares planted with wine grapes, pistachios, walnuts and almonds. The company mechanically harvests its entire nut crop and 50 per cent of the wine crop. To maintain ideal fertilizing and irrigation conditions, it routinely analyses plant tissue for nutrients and measures soil moisture with a special electronic device. TAP also maximizes its use of equipment. Because of the farm's size, fewer machines per hectare are needed to work the land.

A creation of high finance that would dumbfound even a sophisticated family farmer, TAP is the offspring of a larger corporation, which owns property, oil reserves and other businesses. Through the help of this parent company, TAP was able to commit large amounts of capital to the farm. And unlike many individual farmers, it could afford to wait the eight to 10 years necessary to see a reasonable profit on that investment. TAP had a further advantage; it could employ experts in cost accounting, entomology and field-crew management to monitor expenses, fight pests and increase efficiency. Most family farmers must take on such onerous tasks themselves or hire expensive consultants.

American farming, in spite of all its amazing productivity, actually constitutes a very small slice of the nation's economy. Agriculture, forestry and fisheries put together account for only about 3 per cent of the country's gross national product.

The biggest sector of the economy—and also the fastest growing—is that of service industries. In 1981, service industries accounted for 67 per cent of America's gross national product. In one service-industry category, eating and drinking places, the increase in the number of jobs from 1970 to 1981 amounted to more than the total 1981 employment in the car and steelmaking industries combined.

Since service industries do not turn out any tangible products—goods—some people wonder whether a service-orientated economy can increase its total wealth, or even survive for long. The author Mark Twain pointed out about a hundred years ago that no society could prosper by its people "taking in each other's washing". John Nevin, Chairman of The Firestone Tire & Rubber Company, recently restated Mark Twain's viewpoint in modern terms: "The idea that we can have an economy by selling hamburgers to each other is absurd."

Services, in fact, are much bigger than that. They include businesses such as insurance and banking, which accumulate funds that can be invested in manufacturing companies. Other service industries—mail-order houses, department stores and supermarket chains—are essential to the distribution and selling of the goods produced by manufacturers. Services such as health care (a $287-billion-a-year business in 1981) and education ($181-billion-a-year in 1981) assist American productivity in all industries by keeping managers and workers well, and by preparing their children for life in an increasingly complex economy.

The service industries that play the most important role in the American economy are those that come under the general heading of marketing. This category embraces all the business activities involved in directing the flow of goods and services to consumers and other users, from transportation and

At Chicago's huge O'Hare Airport, an airliner taxies on a ramp built over a motorway. O'Hare has so much air traffic that, on average, a plane lands or takes off every 52 seconds.

THE NEW HIGH STREET

Three decades ago shopping centres were rarities. Where they existed at all, they tended to be small. Today there are more than 23,000, covering an average of 12,700 square metres each and annually ringing up $416 billion in retail sales. Once restricted to the suburbs, they now appear in the heart of cities like Washington, D.C., with its Victorian-style Georgetown Park *(left)*.

The secret of their success has perhaps as much to do with their entertainment value as it does with the convenience of having dozens of shops under one roof and a place to park as well. They are airily designed, with wide corridors, open areas, plants and plenty of benches for the tired to rest their feet. And they offer a variety of diversions, from cinemas, restaurants and skating rinks to arts, crafts and antique shows. They are places, as a new word has it, to go malling— to mosey, to see and be seen, to while away an hour or two among other human beings. Indeed, they have all but replaced the high street as America's marketplace and Saturday hang-out.

Teenagers love them and congregate in them, and many of the elderly have made of them a second home. One old-timer, likening the mall he and his friends frequent almost every day to the general store of the past commented: "Instead of sitting around the pot-bellied stove, we have various places where we cluster, and we visit."

Built on three levels around a skylit patio whose feature is an elaborate fountain, Georgetown Park in Washington, D.C., attracts hundreds of thousands of customers a year to its more than 80 stores and restaurants.

warehousing to advertising and accepting the customer's money in a retail store. An estimated one third to one half of the U.S. labour force is employed in some phase of marketing.

A substantial portion of the money spent on marketing goes to advertising. Advertising has been a fact of economic life since Babylonian merchants put up signs describing their wares 5,000 years ago. But no other economy has ever been as advertising-oriented as that of the U.S., where $60 billion were spent on advertisements in 1981. Studies indicate that the average American consumer is exposed to approximately 1,500 ads each day, and actually takes mental note of about 75 of these. By and large, Americans, including the many children who watch commercial television for hours on end, are fairly discriminating, even cynical, about most advertising, extracting whatever information they want from it and mentally thumbing their noses when confronted by oversell.

Like it or not, Americans are stuck with advertising, and have been since the middle of the 19th century, when factories started turning out more goods than could be sold by traditional, leisurely methods of marketing. For advertising is not simply the oil of the U.S. economic machine; it is the power that drives it. As an advertising textbook so candidly puts it: "The mass production of products and services requires constant selling pressure to keep consumption high."

American advertising has spread well beyond its shores, as have various other services, earning foreign exchange that improves the country's balance of payments and thus its ability to buy desirable products from abroad. Exportable services include not only obvious foreign-currency earners such as airlines, but various kinds of financial services and even the sale of hamburgers, as has been demonstrated by a man named Ray Kroc.

When Kroc founded McDonald's Hamburgers in 1955, he launched a new American service industry, the fast-food business. Today, fast-food providers like McDonald's and its proliferating competitors make inexpensive meals easily accessible to virtually all Americans. Fast-food hamburgers, pizzas, fried chicken and even Chinese pancake rolls now amount to a $25-billion-a-year industry in the U.S.

In building his business, Kroc relied on clever mass-marketing and advertising techniques. While retaining ownership of some of the outlets, he sold franchises for about three in every four to local entrepreneurs, who built and then operated the restaurants. Kroc supplied the McDonald's name, methods, mass-purchasing power in buying supplies, and nationwide advertising. In return, he received a percentage of each outlet's gross sales.

Kroc also applied the principles of standardization that were developed in mass production. Machines pre-cut the hamburger to precisely 45 grams of beef; computerized deep-fryers ensure that each batch of French fries has the correct crispness; dispensers squeeze out identical dollops of ketchup. Although some Americans resent the homogenization of their culture that McDonald's represents, an estimated 4 per cent of the U.S. population visits a McDonald's on any given day. There are now more than 5,500 McDonald's outlets in the U.S.—and another 1,200 in 29 foreign countries.

Perhaps the most fascinating indication of the expansion of the service economy is the fact that many services operate on behalf of other service industries. Consider the temporary-employment business, with an eight-billion-dollar-a-year turnover which about 70 per cent of all American businesses use annually, when they need extra help but do not wish to increase their permanent payrolls.

The founder of the temporary-help business was Russell Kelly, progenitor of the famous "Kelly girls". Kelly knew a lot about efficiency. As a fiscal-management analyst in the U.S. Army during World War II, he had established a centralized system for speeding up the payment of invoices and the delivery of food. A colleague noted that Kelly "moved food the way General Patton rolled his tanks".

In 1946, Kelly set up an office staffed by two young women with the intention of offering Detroit businesses help with their typing and clerical work. He expected to provide that help in his own office, but quickly found out that the businesses preferred in fact to have the work done on their own premises. He began sending out his "Kelly girls" to fill in for absent secretaries or to augment the client's regular office staff during peak work periods.

Today, Kelly Services, Inc. employs more than 300,000 temporary workers, men as well as women, who operate from more than 500 branch offices in the United States and abroad. They fill more than 100 job classifications, from filing clerk to computer programmer to product demonstrator to registered nurse. The range of specialities reflects the ever-broadening scope of service occupations in an economy whose success now depends on far more than the fertility of farmland or the speed of assembly lines.

HARVEST OF GOOD LIVING

The growth of corporate agriculture does not worry Ben Dieterich, 30, who with his family and one hired hand farms 600 hectares in central Texas. "The family farm is here to stay," he says. "A corporation couldn't make this farm pay; it takes too much overtime."

Dieterich labours from early morning to nightfall (and at harvest, several hours after dark), with enough modern equipment to stock a dealer's showroom—including three tractors, three cultivators and a $70,000 combine harvester. The high cost of machines plus the expense of seed, fertilizer and pesticides make a farm like Dieterich's a capital-intensive, high-risk business. "It takes pretty near half a million dollars just to start," he observes, "and you could almost be wiped out in one bad year." To guard against that, he diversifies his land and effort between wheat, corn and cattle, while his wife, Lou Ann, cultivates a garden that feeds the family all year.

The Dieterichs must pay to lease most of the land they farm (they own 40 hectares) and are paying off some $100,000 in short-term loans for operating capital. But despite the risks and the hard work, says Lou Ann, "farm life is the best life," and Ben agrees. "I don't think I could bear to do anything else," he says. "I love farming."

Behind the ranch-style house the Dieterichs designed for themselves, Lou Ann hangs out the family washing (she has an electric dryer but likes the fresh smell of clothes that have been dried in the sun). "On a farm with three boys," she says, "you have to wash every single day."

In May, a harvest month for winter wheat in Texas, Ben Dieterich shows sons Chris, eight, and Jason, five, how he estimates the grain's moisture content. The crop will be ready to cut only when the sun has dried it sufficiently.

Chris Dieterich *(in cap)* and his brothers feed ground corn to a cow *(foreground)* and a Brahman bull. This unusually gentle bull is one of two the Dieterichs keep for breeding. Calves sired by Brahmans—descended from Indian stock—can withstand pests, disease and Texas heat.

Lou Ann boils plums to make jam. She bottles or freezes some 260 litres of home-grown produce yearly.

Ben washes a truck lent to him for being selected Texas' outstanding Young Farmer in 1982.

At his desk in the kitchen, Ben brings his accounts up to date. He does all the bookkeeping for the farm, having learnt it on his own. The Texas-shaped mirror and other items on the wall commemorate his selection as an outstanding young farmer.

While hired hand José Rodriguez pumps diesel fuel into a tractor, Ben *(left)* performs some last-minute maintenance before the harvest. Ben keeps 4,000 litres of fuel in tanks on the farm, and he and José do all the repair work on the machinery.

From the comfort of his combine harvester's air-conditioned cab, Ben cuts a 6-metre-wide swath across one of his wheat fields. In a 12-hour day he can cover 40 hectares in the machine, which cuts and threshes the grain, then spouts it into a hopper.

Stealing a few hours of relaxation after a hard week of work, Ben and Lou Ann slow-dance to country music at the Melody Ranch, a nightclub in Waco, 30 kilometres from the farm. They go dancing about once a month.

Ben's mother *(above, left)* and father *(above, right)* join the Dieterichs for a lazy Sunday afternoon on the farmhouse driveway, which doubles as a patio. Descended from a German farmer who emigrated to Texas four generations ago, Ben has some 200 relatives living within 30 kilometres.

Jason *(foreground)* and Brandon pedal through puddles, revelling in the wetness and cool air that follow a Texas plains thunderstorm. Behind Jason are the farm's big aluminium equipment shed and a wooden barn used for hay storage.

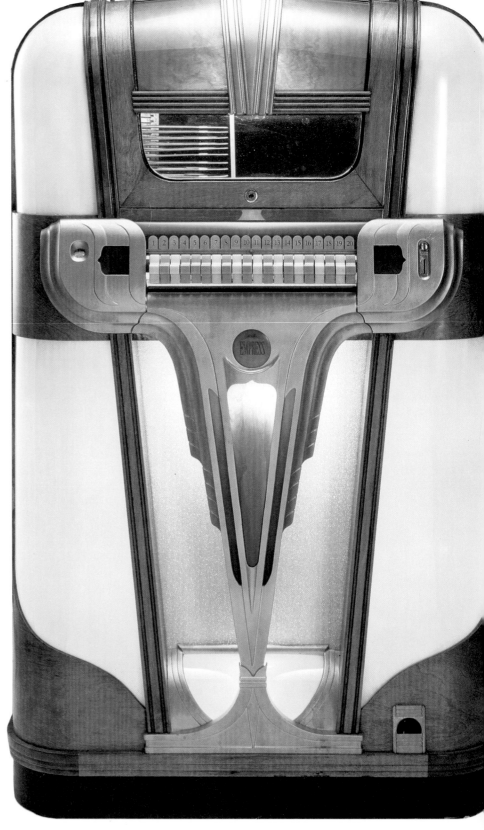

The archetypal artefacts of American popular culture are juke-boxes—coin-in-a-slot gramophones like this 1939 model—that once played in 250,000 bars and cafés across the U.S.

ARTS WITH MASS APPEAL

The country that perfected mass production perhaps inevitably turned assembly-line techniques to the manufacture of mass culture—music, films, television programmes and other forms of entertainment. Many nations made films: Hollywood turned the production of movies into a gigantic industry, at one time the nation's fifth largest in terms of sales. There was an appetite for them. By 1926, scarcely 15 years after the release of the first full-length moving picture, 20,000 cinemas had been built in the U.S. And by the late 1920s, Hollywood was making 700 to 800 films annually.

So it was with music. In 1907, the heyday of sheet-music publishing, 42 songs sold a million or more copies each to customers who took them home to play on the parlour piano. When the phonograph replaced the family piano, record sales became a major American industry. In 1921, a hundred million records were sold in the U.S.; by 1930, however, the figure had plummeted to six million a year.

The villain was radio—another technological advance that spawned a mass-culture industry. There were eight radio stations in 1920; nine years later there were 300. By the early 1930s, a third of all U.S. homes had a radio, providing a potential audience of 60 million for any one programme.

Then along came television, and the hunger for entertainment via the small screen proved insatiable. By the early 1980s, nearly every American household—83 million of them—had at least one television set. To serve the nation's viewers, more than 800 commercial stations had been established around the country, so many that 90 per cent of the viewers could choose from among at least four channels. In addition, by 1983 there were 4,800 cable TV systems catering to 23 million subscribers. And the average household had its set turned on an astonishing six hours and 48 minutes a day.

To keep images flickering non-stop on all those screens, the U.S. television industry was forced to produce many thousands of hours of entertainment in addition to news broadcasts and the re-running of old films. Between the mid-1960s and the early 1980s, the three major networks devoted an average of 1,438 prime-time hours each year to that most characteristic form of American television entertainment, the serial dramatic show. Such continued dramas—along with other American-made programmes—have proved astonishingly popular abroad; by the early 1980s, U.S. television producers were exporting 300,000 hours' worth of programming to stations in more than 100 foreign countries. Critics in some of those nations have cried out at this "cultural imperialism", but their carping only underlines the enormous effect that American popular arts have had around the globe.

America's cultural impact has not of course been confined to the masses. For a nation comparatively so young, the U.S. has cast up an impressive number of recognized masters throughout the arts. The stories and novels of Nathaniel Hawthorne, Herman Melville, Henry James, Edith Wharton and William Faulkner bear comparison with the finest fiction from anywhere. Painting has flourished in the works of the portraitists John Singleton Copley and Thomas Eakins, the watercolours of Winslow Homer and the haunting, realistic canvases of Edward Hopper.

The post-World War II Abstract Expressionist school was the first American-born art movement to exert an international influence. Jackson Pollock, Robert Motherwell and Willem De Kooning became familiar names in art circles the world over. America has given the world great sculptors in Augustus Saint-Gaudens, Alexander Calder, David Smith and Louise Nevelson, and notable composers of classical music in Charles Ives and Aaron Copland.

Yet America's unique contribution to world culture is in the popular realm. Hollywood not only turned film-making into an industry, it also invented several film genres—most notably Western and gangster dramas—that have attracted enormous attention worldwide. Starting from the European operetta, U.S. composers and librettists created an essentially new form of entertainment, the Broadway musical. When African and European musical traditions met in America, they combined to produce a musical expression like no other—jazz, and its outgrowths such as rock and roll.

Mass production of radios and innovations in advertising interacted in the late 1920s to bring forth another native entertainment form, daytime radio

4

A metal "mobile" 26 metres across—
created by U.S. sculptor Alexander
Calder—pivots slowly in the National
Gallery in Washington, D.C. The
National, only one of America's
thousands of museums, welcomes
five million visitors annually.

serials—better known as soap operas or simply "soaps" because the sponsoring advertisers were generally selling cleansing agents. With the coming of television the soaps became visual and even invaded "prime time" programming schedules.

Many of the works turned out by Hollywood and other segments of the huge U.S. entertainment industry have been, despite a high gloss of professionalism, very low on the artistic scale. Yet in the hands of their most gifted creators, the popular arts have on occasion reached the level of high art. These creators, rather than fabricating homogenized products, have put their own ideas and feelings into their works. Instead of exploiting the public, they have tried to communicate with it and, in doing so, have fashioned a surprising number of genuine masterpieces.

One of the greatest of these artists was that blend of suave elegance and musical genius called Duke Ellington. By all odds, he was during his lifetime the most distinguished writer of jazz music, and the most indefatigable. From his first piece in 1923 until his death, of cancer, in 1974, he composed or co-authored more than 1,500 original works, many of them—joyful stomps and moody, poignant laments—embodiments of the essential nature of jazz and of the black experience in America. In company with a handful of gifted instrumentalists such as the trumpeter Louis Armstrong and the pianist Earl Hines, Ellington in the 1920s turned jazz from a mixture of popular and folk music into true art. He pioneered so inventively in musical sounds and forms that all subsequent jazz creators have been in his debt.

When Edward Kennedy Ellington was born, in 1899 in Washington, D.C.,

one of the musical precursors of jazz was already gaining popularity. This was ragtime, a bouncy, lilting type of piano music derived from the quadrille and the march by black musicians in the Mid-west ("ragtime" was a black term for "syncopation"). The most distinguished composer of ragtime was Scott Joplin, a Texan from a poor but musical family. In the year of Ellington's birth, Joplin published his first

work, entitled "Maple Leaf Rag".

This tune, which sold 400,000 copies in sheet music, helped start a ragtime craze that spread from the Mid-west to New Orleans, Baltimore, New York and Washington, as well as abroad. In Washington, while Ellington was growing up, half a dozen black ragtime pianists flourished and the future composer absorbed ragtime's melodies and syncopations—cross rhythms and

polyrhythms that, as musicologist Gunther Schuller maintains, American blacks had retained in their songs and chants from their African homelands.

Ellington grew up as a pampered child—"my parents were very strict," he later joked, "about seeing that I got everything I wanted." His doting mother and father provided early piano instruction—with a teacher who was named, improbably enough, Mrs. Clinkscales—but the lessons did not prosper. "I missed more than I took," Ellington recalled, "because of my enthusiasm for playing ball."

He nevertheless picked up enough knowledge of the piano to begin playing at high-school parties. He picked up more tips on piano technique by watching the pianists who frequented a Washington pool room, where they entertained the pool players. He also—and this was important for his development—heard the piano roll of James P. Johnson's "Carolina Shout" at a friend's house, and spent hours running this breakneck number at slow speed through the piano so that he could follow the great New York pianist's fingering.

Armed with the "Carolina Shout" as his featured piece, Ellington increasingly eschewed baseball for music. By the age of 18, the Duke—as he was called by then, for his elegant dress and bearing—was forming his own small bands and playing at a variety of social functions. So successful did the young musical entrepreneur become that by the time he was 20 he was supporting a wife and a baby son comfortably, and owned his own house and car.

Despite his home-town success, Ellington hankered after the excitement of New York. In 1922 he took the leap, travelling with two fellow musicians to

This starkly graceful combination of moulded plywood and tubular metal is probably the best-known piece of 20th-century American furniture. Designed by Charles Eames in 1946, it has been manufactured in thousands.

what was already the capital of the entertainment industry. But work was hard to find and at first they nearly starved. Eventually, they formed the "Washingtonians" and found a home in the Kentucky Club, a night spot at Broadway and 49th Street. There the band, now augmented by several new members, played for four years—to ever-increasing acclaim.

At the time, several sorts of jazz were heard in New York. There was the home-grown "Harlem Stride" piano music played by Ellington's idol,

James P. Johnson, by Johnson's star pupil, a massive young man named Fats Waller, and by Willie "The Lion" Smith, whose unusual harmonies would permanently influence Ellington's own playing. Added to this were brassy sounds from New Orleans, where another kind of jazz had been born from a cross-fertilization of ragtime and the music of the Crescent City's marching bands *(pages 106–113)*.

A five-piece group made up of white New Orleans musicians, the Original Dixieland Jazz Band, had brought a

version of this music to New York as early as 1917. By the mid-1920s, two superb instrumentalists, Sidney Bechet and Armstrong, had arrived in the city and added their own refined interpretations. Bechet, a clarinetist and soprano saxophonist, for some months blew his soaring, impassioned choruses as a member of Ellington's group at the Kentucky Club. Armstrong impressed every musician in town with the blazing, New Orleans-derived trumpet solos he played during the one year, 1924, that he spent with

4

Fletcher Henderson's orchestra at the Roseland Ballroom in New York.

Then there were the blues, originating in the South and South-west, and sung most memorably by the incomparable Bessie Smith. Her huge, resonant voice, one critic said, had "all the carrying quality (and some of the timbre) of a diesel locomotive horn", and her mesmeric and soulful laments, such as "Empty Bed Blues", defined what the blues could and should be.

All these stirring sounds invigorated Ellington's imagination and they were heard in the music his band was playing. At first, as Sonny Greer, Ellington's drummer, recalled, "Duke wasn't writing so much, but he would take the popular tunes and twist them" so that their small group sounded "like a big band, but soft and beautiful". Soon, however, the Duke was composing original material, some inspired by, and tailored to, the extraordinary muted, growling trumpet playing of Bubber Miley and the equally eerie growls and wails Charlie Irvis could achieve on the trombone. The band's new sound was dubbed the "jungle style" and it remained Ellington's trademark throughout the 1920s.

Ellington really launched his career as a composer, however, when in 1927 his band began a five-year stay at the Cotton Club, then Harlem's flossiest night spot. Ellington was required to write both dance tunes and a variety of production numbers for the shows. He also enlarged the band from six to 11 pieces and, finding himself with an even more richly timbred, various and versatile aggregation than before, began to compose original numbers that would exploit its musical resources.

Part of Ellington's genius went into forming this orchestra, which, in the

words of photographer and writer Gordon Parks, could "unfold softly like a flower or explode like a bomb". Largely because it was the medium through which he expressed himself, the Duke kept his orchestra together for 50 years, with many of the key men staying on for most of those decades.

For them Ellington wrote his famous melodies—"Sophisticated Lady", "Mood Indigo", "Solitude", "Don't Get Around Much Any More"—and what can only be called swinging concertos that evoke a train ride ("Daybreak Express") or the sounds of a noisy tenement ("Harlem Air Shaft"). In these and others, such as "Morning Glory", "Ko-Ko" and "Conga Bra-

va", Ellington's writing and the band's playing produced what critic Whitney Balliett has called "a rending, incredibly rich sound that is one of the delights of Western orchestral music".

Despite the exhaustions of non-stop composing and long trips with the orchestra—to every corner of the country and to many different parts of Europe—Ellington remained always the same: unruffled, urbane, dressed with impeccable taste. He was admired by blacks as an entertainer who was always dignified. "Ellington never grinned," Gordon Parks remembered. "He smiled. Ellington never shuffled. He strode. It was 'Good afternoon ladies and gentlemen', never 'How y'all

96

doin'?'' To Parks and other young blacks, Ellington was "elegant, handsome and awe-inspiring".

The Duke was as spirited, witty and inventive in his speech as he was in his music. When someone remarked that his gifted assistant arranger and all-round collaborator Billy Strayhorn, whom the Duke called "Swee' Pea", was "Ellington's alter ego", the Duke slyly protested. "Let's not go overboard. Pea is only my right arm, left foot, eyes, stomach, ears and soul, not my ego." His charm was such that he could tell a woman, "I knew you were here because the whole studio was suddenly aglow with a turquoise radiance"—and get away with it.

During the Swing Era of the 1930s and early 1940s, Ellington and his band were never as popular with the dancing public as the slicker, more musically predictable orchestras of Tommy Dorsey, Benny Goodman and Count Basie. Because he and his men were black, many hotel ballrooms and other prestigious auditoriums banned them for many years. Asked about this, Ellington gave a characteristically wry answer: "I took the energy it takes to pout and wrote some blues."

But eventually the recognition the Duke deserved came his way. He was awarded at least 15 honorary doctoral degrees by U.S. colleges and universities, given the keys to 13 American cities and the Presidential Medal of Freedom, the nation's highest civilian award. But perhaps Ellington's ultimate reward was the pleasure he took in his own work—and in seeing others the world over enjoy it too.

The rhythms and sounds of ragtime and jazz strongly influenced the originators of the Broadway musical, another indigenous American creation, and

gave their shows much of their spark and appeal. It was no accident that one of the first songs written by a Manhattan singing waiter named Israel Baline—better known as Irving Berlin—was titled "Alexander's Ragtime Band", or that one of the first numbers George Gershwin wrote with his lyricist brother Ira began, "The real American folksong is a rag."

American musical comedies were the product in part of European operettas with their gossamer-thin plots and romantic music, and in part of such native-born entertainments as theatrical revues and vaudeville. The impresario Florenz Ziegfeld staged revues that he called the *Follies* year after year, and he was rivalled in the early 1920s by producer George White's *Scandals* and by Irving Berlin's *Music Box Revues*. In the mid-1920s, the operetta and the theatrical revue coalesced in a new and delicious confection, the musical play.

Most of the earliest musicals had plots as thin as the airiest operetta. The Gershwins' first major success, *Oh, Kay!* (1926), was a bit of Prohibition-era nonsense about an impoverished English lord who sets out to restore the family fortunes by bootlegging liquor from his yacht to the shores of Long Island. But it was the songs that George and Ira hung on such shaky plot lines that enchanted the original audiences and still delight the listener today.

George's dazzlingly fertile musical imagination poured out several hundred such melodies. He also found time to write longer symphonic compositions such as his jazz-based *Rhapsody in Blue* and *Concerto in F*, as well as his opera, *Porgy and Bess*. Even before his tragically premature death at the age of 38 in 1937 of a brain tumour, Gershwin was hailed by some critics as the greatest of all American composers.

Virtually all of the musicals produced in the 1920s and 1930s were giddily plotted excuses for good songs, sprightly dance numbers, a bit of romance and some comedy routines. But then in December 1927, a musical arrived on Broadway that would help to shatter this tradition. It was called *Show Boat*, with music by Jerome Kern and lyrics by Oscar Hammerstein II. When the curtains parted on the opening night, there were no giddy singing-and-dancing chorus girls, but a group of black dockers soulfully lamenting the drudgery of lifting back-breaking bales of cotton. As the story unfolded, it became clear that the songs were not simply charming interludes. Hammerstein's lyrics advanced the plot and explained character, and Kern's music reinforced the mood. This new element of seriousness and unification of song and story captured theatre-goers' imaginations. *Show Boat* became such a hit that after its New York run, it toured the country for seven months.

Another major breakthrough occurred in 1940 with Richard Rodgers' and Lorenz Hart's *Pal Joey*. The musical was something of an anti-romance; the hero was a callous con man and gigolo, but this did not make the team's songs any less memorable or delightful. Hart was one of the greatest masters of comic rhyme since Lord Byron wrote *Don Juan*, and *Pal Joey* is full of them. Lamenting her infatuation with the faithless Joey, the play's heroine opines that she is "wild again!/Beguiled again!/A simpering, whimpering child again!" Then she adds that "A pill he is,/But still he is/All mine and I'll keep him until he is/Bewitched, bothered and bewildered/Like me!"

After that show, musicals gained a

new maturity, a new co-ordination between libretto, tunes, lyrics and even ballet-like dance numbers that also served to help tell the story. One of the masters of the new musical was Cole Porter, who, like Berlin, wrote the lyrics for his own songs. In his most insouciant and sophisticated show, *Kiss me, Kate*, virtually every song contributes directly to furthering the plot or giving new depth to the characters.

Words and music are also tightly tied to the story of Frank Loesser's *Guys and Dolls* and Berlin's *Annie Get Your Gun*. But perhaps the masterpieces of the genre are *My Fair Lady*, the superb musical version of George Bernard Shaw's play *Pygmalion*, by Alan Jay Lerner and Frederick Loewe; and *Oklahoma!* and *South Pacific*, two works by Richard Rodgers and Oscar Hammerstein II. In them all, music and words, plot and dance, setting and action are so completely married to each other that something close to a new and utterly beguiling form of theatrical art was the result.

Long before this post-World War II apotheosis of the musical took place, while jazz and other forms of 20th-century popular music were in their infancy, another popular art to which the U.S. made crucial and original contributions was coming of age: the cinema. For 40 years, beginning in about 1920, films were the dominant form of mass entertainment in America. Indeed, for millions of American citizens, they were the only form of dramatic entertainment. So pervasive, so powerful was the effect of films on the American public that they did not so much mirror life, as life mirrored the films. When in the romantic comedy *It Happened One Night* Clark Gable undressed to reveal that he wore no vest, the shop sales of

such garments plummeted across the entire nation.

For all practical purposes, the American movie was born in 1903 in Thomas A. Edison's laboratories in New Jersey, where a cameraman named Edwin Porter created *The Great Train Robbery*, an eight-minute film that electrified the public and also introduced several motifs that would characterize many American films to come. It was a Western, its cast was made up of easily recognized good guys and bad, and it introduced the speed and suspense of the chase scene.

The next great step was taken in 1915 when a former actor named David Wark Griffith produced his epic *Birth of a Nation*, which chronicled the Civil War era and the rise of the Ku Klux Klan during the Reconstruction period. Lasting an unheard-of three hours, Griffith's drama revolutionized filmmaking around the world. "It established," said one film historian, "the immense power of the medium to produce extended emotional and psychological effects."

It was in the realm of film comedy, however, that early American filmmakers truly led the world. The first and still unchallenged king of comedy was a frustrated singer from East Berlin, Connecticut, named Mack Sennett, who, although he mass-produced his two-reel farces, achieved in many of them a sublime poetry of comic chaos. Beginning in 1909, Sennett scoured America's circuses and burlesque and vaudeville houses for the best and the broadest slapstick comedians he could find. He formed them into a repertory company that featured the Keystone Kops, seven of the most insanely incompetent policemen ever seen on earth. The Kops inevitably became

ADORED RELICS OF ELVIS

In the decades after World War II, a musical mania called rock and roll—a thumping, shouting, twanging outgrowth of jazz—swept through the U.S. and then the world. The unquestioned monarch of rock—at least until England's Beatles adapted the music—was a former lorry driver named Elvis Presley. So adored was Elvis by his millions of fans that, since his death of a heart attack at the age of 42 in 1977, such artefacts as his cars have been treasured with almost religious awe.

Rock and roll was created by black musicians in the late 1930s, and it appealed almost exclusively to a black audience—until Elvis. Born in Tupelo, Mississippi, and raised in Memphis, Tennessee, he borrowed the rhythmic drive and vocal intonations of the largely Southern black rockers, popularizing the music and vastly broadening its audience. His first major record, "Heartbreak Hotel", sold three million copies. Within two years Presley had grossed $100 million. By 1968, 200 million of his records had sold and he had appeared in 29 films—at an average fee of $850,000 each.

A good measure of Presley's huge popularity could be attributed to the wild physical gyrations—he was dubbed "Elvis the Pelvis"—that accompanied his singing. To his teenage fans, his movements and rich voice spoke of sex, independence and revolt against authority. Yet Elvis appears to have been an ill-adjusted and fearful man who at the height of his fame—and despite his enormous wealth—became a near-recluse in his Memphis mansion, where he retreated further into the drug use that seems to have hastened his premature death.

A plaster portrait of Presley *(right)*, one of the millions of Elvis images made during his lifetime, stares out from a shop window. It emphasizes the hooded eyes and brooding look that entranced his female fans.

The interior of Presley's favourite Cadillac *(below)* has electric shoe-shining equipment, a record player, a television and a make-up mirror—appurtenances mostly finished in 24-carat gold plate. The car is preserved in a museum in Nashville, Tennessee, the centre of another native American musical form, country and western.

The exterior of the same $100,000 Cadillac gleams with 40 coats of hand-rubbed lacquer. It is painted, in the words of the man who made the custom fitting, "gold-dust white".

4

embroiled with some equally crazy male civilians and with Sennett's troupe of Bathing Beauties, a gaggle of hearty young women in disconcerting knee-length swimsuits. "All these people," wrote James Agee, the critic and film writer *(The African Queen)*, "zipped and caromed about the pristine world of the screen as jazzily as a convention of water bugs. Words can hardly suggest how energetically they collided and bounced apart, meeting in full gallop around the corner of a house; how hard and how often they fell on their backsides; or with what fantastically adroit clumsiness they got themselves fouled up in folding ladders, garden hoses, tethered animals and each other's headlong cross-purposes."

Sennett perfected the chase sequence, and virtually all of his farces end with the Kops and others in pell-mell pursuit of some fleeing scapegoat who has aroused their anger. Sennett's chases built up "such a majestic trajectory of pure anarchic motion," Agee wrote, "that bathing girls, cops, comics, dogs, cats, babies, automobiles, locomotives, innocent bystanders, sometimes what seemed like a whole city, an entire civilization, were hauled along head over heels in the wake of that energy like dry leaves following an express train."

Sennett claimed to have originated the technique of speeding up the action of silent comedies by cranking the camera too slowly. When the film was shown by a normal-speed projector, the action became faster and fizzier than real life. He also fostered the development of that archetypal comic device, the custard pie in the face.

The apex of the art was reached, however, in a two-reeler by Sennett's rival, Hal Roach, featuring the comic team of Stan Laurel and Oliver Hardy. Early in the film a bakery van is parked in the middle of a street scene, providing limitless ammunition for the battle to come. Laurel and Hardy begin the pie throwing, of course, but ultimately a dozen passers-by become involved; the finale is a custard Armageddon with dozens, hundreds, of pies flying through the air.

Sennett and Roach and other makers of Hollywood comedy did not strive consciously for artistic form. Their consuming aim was simply to delight film audiences by reducing them to helpless laughter. But they achieved on occasion a pure and innocent perfection of comic art, piling one hilarious device upon another to reach a crescendo of frenzied motion.

Another of Sennett's contributions to comedy was to nurture the talents of a pair of comedians who would raise silent comedy to new levels of artistry, Charles Chaplin and Buster Keaton. An English music-hall comedian who made 30 films for Sennett before going on his own, Chaplin early created his immortal tramp. Dressed in ill-fitting clothes—oversized trousers and undersized jacket and bowler—Chaplin's waif became the eternal victim of manic fold-out beds, whirling revolving doors and ultimately, modern mechanical society as a whole. The figure of the tramp became as familiar around the world as Mickey Mouse *(opposite page)* and equally loved.

In his fine longer films such as *City Lights* and *The Gold Rush*, Chaplin could combine pathos—always inherent in the tramp figure—and even tragedy with his inspired slapstick. In *City Lights* the tramp has somehow found the money to help a blind flower girl have an operation that restores her sight. She has imagined her benefactor as princely, not as an absurd semi-outcast. The tramp for his part has never realized his own inadequacies. Then, no longer blind, she sees the tramp for the first time. As Agee describes the scene: "She recognizes who he must be by his shy, confident, shining joy as he comes silently toward her. And he recognizes himself, for the first time, through the terrible changes in her face." It is a scene, Agee concludes, that can "shrivel the heart to see, and it is the greatest piece of acting and the highest moment in movies."

Keaton's comedy was also refined and subtle, but in a different way. After playing in several Keystone efforts, he produced on his own a sequence of two dozen or so superb films that include some of the most deft and preposterous—but also strangely moving—comic sequences ever invented.

Keaton, born in 1895, was already playing the part of a human volleyball in his parents' rough-and-tumble vaudeville act at the age of three and a half. Part of the comedy came from the boy's ability to hurtle about the stage without changing expression; ever after, he was "The Great Stone Face", meeting all crises with a mask as fixed and haunting as an old daguerreotype.

When he came to make his own films in 1920, Keaton was the past master at slipping on banana skins and every other gesture in the vocabulary of silent comedy. He went on to elaborate and refine them with unparalleled inventiveness. His *Cops* is one long chase, but here Keaton is pursued not by half a dozen incompetent Keystoners, but by an entire metropolitan police force with hundreds of cops snatching at his coat-tails. In *Sherlock Jr.* he engineers a superb variant on the chase sequence,

AN EMPIRE BUILT BY A MOUSE

Mickey and Pluto confer eye-to-eye in "The Pointer", a 1939 cartoon about hunting.

One of the century's most celebrated personalities has been that amiable rodent, Mickey Mouse, created by Walter Elias Disney. The huge company built on Mickey's fame must be judged the leading purveyor of mass entertainment in U.S. history.

Disney's early years gave little promise of his later achievements. He left school at the age of 15 to become a commercial artist in Kansas City, but success eluded him. When he went to Hollywood in 1923 to try making animated cartoons, all he took with him were drawing skills and the memory of a friendly mouse that had shared his studio. After another five hungry years, Disney remembered his furry companion and he made him the hero of a crude cartoon called *Steamboat Willie*.

Mickey was an instant success, as were the playmates Disney soon gave him, such as the irascible Donald Duck and the faithful hound Pluto. When the costs of making short cartoons rose sharply and reduced profits, he cannily began producing high-profit feature-length animated films. The first, *Snow White*, grossed eight million dollars on its initial release in 1937, earning more than any other film up to that date. Other productions were almost as profitable. By the mid-1950s Disney had made 657 films, seen by an estimated one billion people.

And he was far from finished. During the 1950s he began turning out adventure films with live actors as well as nature films such as *The Living Desert*—which cost $300,000 to make and took in five million dollars worldwide. In addition, before his death in 1966, Disney created two successful amusement parks, Disneyland in California and Disney World in Florida.

Disney's friends and associates have agreed that his success arose from his ceaseless energy and his ability to retain the outlook of a child. He looked at the world, said the artist Salvador Dali, "with uncontaminated wonder." Disney had his own view: "We're selling corn, and I like corn."

hurtling dizzily through crowded rush-hour traffic on the handlebars of a motorcycle, unaware that the driver has been left behind.

He was also a master at twisting impossible situations. As an early Christian martyr thrown into a lion's den, he plays Androcles and removes a thorn from the lion's paw. Then, in a lovely parody of a manicurist's routine, he polishes the complaisant beast's claws.

Through all his trials Keaton remained undefeated. Chaplin wrung pathos from the defeats and humiliations suffered by his tramp, but in Keaton's films there is no sentimentality. Behind that stoic mask there is always an unconquerable will to survive, even to triumph.

While Keaton, Chaplin and their fellow masters of silent comedy were developing and refining their art, other U.S. film-makers were inventing and elaborating other uniquely American genres of film—the Western, then the gangster epic and later, after the coming of sound to pictures, the filmed musical comedy. Of them all, the most enduringly popular, both in the United States and around the world, has been the Western. To many of the world's filmgoers, America *is* the West as shown in these films, a huge, empty land across which desperadoes, bands of whooping Indians and lone gunfighters eternally gallop.

The U.S. film industry began to make Westerns right from the start. The pioneering director D.W. Griffith filmed a number of short Westerns, starting as early as 1908. Since then, so many have been produced that an estimated one quarter of all films ever made in the U.S. have been Westerns.

Their universal and lasting appeal has certainly been partly due to the

John Wayne, the archetypal he-man Western hero, uses his fists on Montgomery Clift in a rousing 1948 film, *Red River*. It was directed by Howard Hawks, one of the two—with John Ford—most admired makers of classic Westerns.

films' sheer excitement—the gunplay, the breakneck horseback pursuits, the careening stagecoaches under attack by Indians or outlaws. But there is also the nostalgia they bring for what seems a better, simpler time. The date in Westerns is always about 1870; the dramas are set in a pristine world, unfouled by cities and beyond the trammels of civilization. It is a world where right and wrong, the good guys and the bad, are always clearly identified.

Still another reason the public has loved Westerns is their ritualistic quality, familiar settings and virtually identical casts of characters. The usual scene is a dusty frontier town with a bank, sheriff's office and saloon and dance hall. Equally familiar are the town's inhabitants, who include, in one critic's list, "the sheriff, the doctor, the prostitute, the telegrapher, the saloon keeper and the quiet, mysterious stranger who wanders in and may be the fastest gun alive". The filmgoer also recognizes "the hired killer, the ranching baron, the cardsharp, and the itinerant potion-vendor", and understands "the rituals of the posse, the hanging party, the cavalry rescue" and "the shoot-out on the main street".

The focus of the drama is, of course, the "mysterious stranger", the gunfighter, the Westerner himself. It is in him—the furious action and the rituals aside—that the main appeal of the Western film resides. Some of the attractions of this hero are obvious: he is tall, self-contained to the point of silence, rides a horse faultlessly, employs his pistols only reluctantly but then better than anyone else—and, as critic Robert Warshow has noted, "can keep his countenance in the face of death".

His appeal is even deeper. Unlike the average man or woman, he does not seem to need to make a living, much less "get ahead" in the world. If he is acting as the town sheriff, he gets paid, but no amount of money could be sufficient recompense for the risks he takes. When asked why he must defy seemingly certain death to defeat the villains, he is likely to explain simply that he "has to do it".

In the final analysis, what the hero must perform is a self-assigned duty. What he defends, as Warshow has put it, is "the purity of his own image—in fact, his honour". In short, Western films and their heroes have probably derived much of their enormous appeal from the fact that they satisfy deep, unspoken desires in their audiences—a longing to believe that they too could show such courage under pressure, that worldly success is not the most important thing in life, that the concept of personal honour still has validity.

So popular is the genre that filmmakers in such unlikely places as Japan, Germany, India, Italy and even

Ginger Rogers and Fred Astaire, the most brilliant dance team to grace that peculiarly American art form, the film musical, whirl through one of their celebrated numbers, "The Yam", in the 1938 film *Carefree*. The duo appeared together in 10 films.

the Soviet Union have made their own Westerns. At their worst these films have been mere pastiches of the original. And yet they have been amazingly profitable. If imitation is the sincerest form of flattery, nothing could more dramatically demonstrate the vast appeal of this peculiarly American form of film drama than these foreign rehashes of the genre.

While European directors and producers kept on making their Westerns, Hollywood's own production of Western films—and other sorts of films as well—slowed to a crawl under the impact of that great post-World War II revolution in the entertainment industry, television. In 1947, cinema attendance in the U.S. averaged 90 million a week. By 1957, this was halved. Meanwhile the number of television sets shot from 16,000 in 1947 to 33 million in 1955 and 142 million by the early 1980s, with more than 340 million elsewhere around the world.

The Western formula proved its perennial appeal in the new medium; a dozen of television's most popular dramatic shows were Westerns. Television, with its all-consuming appetite, also adapted other forms of entertainment. One was a uniquely American type of radio drama, the soap opera, which had been entrancing millions of housewives and other devotees on weekday afternoons since the invention of the soaps in the late 1920s.

Detailing the adventures of all manner of imaginary characters, from small-town folk to big-city theatre people, the daily 15-minute radio dramas followed a formula best described by the humorist James Thurber. "A soap opera is a kind of sandwich," Thurber wrote. "Between thick slices of advertising spread twelve minutes of dialogue, add predicament, villainy and female suffering in equal measure, throw in a dash of nobility, sprinkle with tears, season with organ music, cover with a rich announcer sauce, and serve fives times a week."

Considering the predictability of the formula, it is not surprising that soap operas seldom if ever reached even the lowest level of artistic value, but their production established new records for dramatic mass manufacture. Among the originators of the soap opera were a Chicago husband-and-wife team, Frank and Anne Hummert, who for a time tapped out thousands of words each week to keep their initial shows supplied with plots and dialogue. Soon, however, the Hummerts formed a corporation and hired a stable of

4

"dialoguers" (in the trade's jargon) to turn out episodes at $125 a week. At one time in the mid-1930s the Hummerts had 67 shows on the air each week, worth nine million dollars in advertisers' money per year. As early as 1938 their serials had totalled five million words—about 55 full-length novels.

The all-time champion at producing scripts for the radio soaps appears to have been a former Chicago newspaperman named Robert Douglas Hardy Andrews, who was one of the first writers hired by the Hummerts. A tall, 90-kilogram man with strong wrists and an apparently indestructible typewriter, Andrews quickly hit his stride, turning out five 15-minute scripts a day. Fuelled daily by 40 cups of coffee, he averaged for some years 100,000 words per week and on one occasion, when a number of scripts were required in a special hurry, produced 32,000 words in 20 hours.

The soap opera architect and writer who had the greatest staying power, however, was Irna Phillips, an Ohio schoolteacher who in 1930, at the age of 28, went to Chicago and got herself a job dialoguing the early episodes of a soap called *Today's Children*. Within a few years, Irna Phillips had become the undisputed Queen of the Soaps, and she remained so for 40 years, until her death in 1973. She invented and wrote several of the most popular of all the serials, including *The Guiding Light* and *As the World Turns*. At her peak in the mid-1930s she was regularly turning out 60,000 words per week and earning a handsome $250,000 a year or even more—in pre-World War II dollars.

Irna Phillips' own interests and anxieties influenced the content of her serials and, because they proved popular, many other soaps as well. Her memor-

The cast of the television programme *M*A*S*H* gathers around Alan Alda *(standing, third from left)*, who acted in every episode and directed and wrote some of the best. The show, which lasted longer than the Korean War it dramatized, was nominated for 99 of TV's Emmy Awards and won 14.

ies of her small-town, family-oriented childhood encouraged her to put the challenges and troubles of everyday family life at the centre of most of her creations. She was haunted by the fear of illness and was fascinated by doctors. As a result her characters, and those of her many followers, were frequently afflicted by bizarre and terrible diseases, and were tended to by legions of glamorous medics.

When television came along, a number of Phillips' soaps easily made the transition to being seen as well as heard. For a time in the mid-1970s her *As the World Turns*, by then carried on by her most successful disciple, Agnes Nixon, was among the most popular of all television shows, and Agnes Nixon's own *Search for Tomorrow* ranked as the longest-running show of any sort being shown on television.

By the late 1970s, the soaps were having a further impact on television scheduling and on the viewing habits of millions that Irna Phillips perhaps never foresaw. The essential Phillipsian formula—the tribulations of a family continued with many variations week after week—had been adapted to evening, or "prime-time", dramas.

The most popular of these hour-long, once-a-week serial epics was *Dallas*, a riveting saga of lust and greed among the members of a Texas oil family. By the early 1980s the villainies of the ruthless antihero, J.R. Ewing, had become so irresistible that 40 million Americans were watching the show every week. It proved so popular in other parts of the world that it was being exported to 57 countries; for a time the rage for *Dallas* reached such proportions in Britain that 30 million people, more than half the population, tuned in for key episodes in the drama.

Television gave new life and vibrancy not only to soap operas, but also to the comedy programmes that had been staple of radio. The most popular of these was a show featuring a tall, redheaded actress who had played a number of wise-cracking parts in films, Lucille Ball.

In 1951, Ball and her then-husband, a Cuban-born bandleader named Desi Arnaz, decided to find out what this new medium of television was all about. The Columbia Broadcasting System had asked her to come up with a comedy show that would be similar to one she had done on radio called *My Favorite Husband*. Ball and Arnaz concocted a story about a dizzy but endearing redhead who was married—of course—to a Cuban bandleader. Borrowing $5,000, they rented a Californian film studio, hired a cameraman and made the pilot show themselves.

The result was *I Love Lucy*. At the end of its first six months it was drawing the largest-ever TV audience, and within two years Ball and Arnaz signed a contract for eight million dollars to continue producing and acting in it.

The success of *I Love Lucy* and its sequel, *The Lucy Show*, was its uncanny ability to adapt the formats of earlier radio comedy programmes to television, and its charm was largely the result of Ball's combining this comedy with slapstick of a sort, including custard pies, that dated back to silent comedy. In *I Love Lucy*, the characters were faced each week with a problem that would intensify and ultimately get out of control until a rather improbable solution occurred. But despite the broad and outlandish comedy, Lucy remained a wholly sympathetic figure. The show went on and on, its popularity undimmed after 20 years. It has been dubbed into dozens of languages.

I Love Lucy gave rise to a wealth—some might say a plague—of similar comedies on television, a genre that soon gained the name of "situation comedy", or "sitcom". Few have had anything like the zip and sizzle of the Lucy shows. But a few have managed to portray characters recognizable as real people, and one or two have reached, improbably, something that could be called art, combining with their comedy a sense of reality and an appreciation of the complexity of human life.

The most compelling of these sitcoms seemed at first an unlikely candidate indeed. It was about a U.S. Army surgical unit during the Korean War—a group of doctors and nurses doing a grim job in a war-torn corner of the earth. Yet *M*A*S*H* became a signpost of what television at its best could be. Despite the rapid-fire quips of the surgeons Hawkeye and Trapper John—and *M*A*S*H* could be very funny—it did not gloss over the horrors of war, and all the characters, as week after week of the show went on, came to have unsuspected depths, unforeseen strengths and unexpected vulnerabilities. It became, as one critic mourning its last show in 1983 put it, "the most intelligent, passionate, imaginative and fiercely funny comedy series in the history of U.S. television."

As so often in matters of popular culture, the importance of an achievement can be measured in numbers. When *M*A*S*H* finally went off the air after 11 years and 251 episodes, the rate for a 30-second commercial had climbed to the stunning figure of $200,000. But *M*A*S*H* was able to tap the wallets of advertisers only because it had touched something important in the make-up of its viewers—very possibly their hearts.

Fans applaud the Humphrey brothers' band, one of four rotating groups that nightly draw crowds of jazz lovers to Preservation Hall in the French Qua

SOUND OF A CITY'S SOUL

Jazz emerged in New Orleans at the dawn of this century, and within a few decades it had spread around the world. But this uniquely American art form never really left home; it is still ingrained in the soul of the city. Jazz bursts from the doorways of Bourbon Street bars, pours from radios, enlivens parades, ennobles funerals. An estimated half of the 1,600 members of the local musicians' union are jazzmen, an impressive percentage in a city that embraces all kinds of music, from rock to symphonic.

And the city embraces all shades of jazz, too, from the slickly commercial to the avant-garde. But there is plenty of the purely traditional kind. Its practitioners include the combos at Preservation Hall (average age, 70-plus) and the schoolchildren learning the art from men who studied with the pupils of such greats as Lorenzo Tio Jr., Big Eye Louis Nelson, Alphonse Picou, Peter Bocage and George Baquet. Gaps in the ranks are quickly filled by eager young players carrying on a tradition now four generations old.

Night spots lining Bourbon Street blaze with light and pulse with sound. Here, on a corner of St. Peter Street, the Maison Bourbon proclaims its dedication to preserving jazz.

On Royall Street, young feet trip to the old-time beat of the French Market Jazz Band. The front man's sombrero does double duty as collection plate.

Jazz musician Charles Beasley and his son, aged five, stage a riverside trumpet duet. The Mississippi paddle-steamer behind them recalls days when such craft first carried jazz north.

New Orleans children take to jazz at an early age. These youngsters are playing at McDonogh School No. 15, where jazz is taught as a regular part of the music curriculum.

In a New Orleans custom older than
the century, a marching band plays
solemn music at the outset of a
funeral procession. A member of a
fraternal order leads the way in
sequined sash and gloves, his white-
plumed fan beneath his arm.

With whistle blasts and fan flourishes,
a "captain" calls the tunes on the way
back from the burial. The pace
quickens to the beat of numbers like
"Didn't He Ramble", and spectators
form a joyous, dancing "second line"
right behind the band.

Preston Jackson plays alone in the courtyard of his Orleans Street home. Born in 1902, he left New Orleans at 15, played with various legendary jazz figures and in the mid-1970s revisited and fell under the spell of his native city, where he remained, because "I began to like what I saw."

Assemblyman Solomon Blatt ponders
a point in his law office in Barnwell,
South Carolina. Most state assemblies
meet only one month a year, but
legislators like Blatt must contend
with demands from voters all year.

THE POWER STRUCTURE

When speaking of "the system", an American is probably discussing politics and about to complain. "The system" is conversational shorthand for the forces, official and unofficial, that run the United States, whether at the local, the state or the national level.

Political power, vested by the Constitution in the people, derives in practice from the interaction of these forces and the constituencies they represent. In some instances the constituency may be the voters of a town or a congressional district. In others it might be a special-interest group: a labour union or a corporation or a local civic organization made up of home owners who do not want a sewage-treatment plant built in their neighbourhood.

The system, most Americans will readily avow, is far from perfect and often somewhat less than democratic. But in its own lumbering and cumbersome way, it usually gets the job done. That the system is imperfect and that it works anyway, often surprisingly well, may be the only two sweeping statements about it that would enjoy the concurrence of almost all Americans. Almost anything else that one might say—about who constitutes the U.S. power structure, about how and why it functions, about the nature of its major shortcomings—can be expected to meet substantial disagreement from one quarter or another.

The basic framework and processes of the federal government *(page 118)* are clearly delineated in the Constitution, and the structures of state and local governments are similar to the federal model. However, only schoolchildren or the most naive of adult Americans would contend that the nation (or any particular state or town in it) is run solely by elected and duly appointed officials performing their Constitutionally defined roles and keeping the best interests of the whole electorate always uppermost in their minds.

Most people take it for granted that a multitude of other individuals and institutions—publicly recognized or shadowy, selfish or altruistic, righteous or nefarious—continually affect the course of government.

Consider, for instance, the news media. Those who are part of this institution—reporters, editors, television newscasters, owners of newspapers—generally believe that they have a special role in the system. They consider themselves the watchdogs of society, the protectors of the public's right to know what is going on, not only in government but also in private enterprises whose actions affect the public. But many Americans believe that the news media have arrogated more power to themselves than the Constitution meant them to have and therefore have too much of a hold on the public mind.

So it goes with other elements of the power structure. Environmentalists say that industrial corporations exert too much influence on government and

5

jeopardize the nation's health by polluting air and water. Corporations allege that labour unions damage the economy by demanding exorbitant wages. Labour unions contend that environmentalists care more about recreation for the well-to-do than about jobs for workers. Some civil libertarians say that churches are too powerful and that they contrive to impose private morals on public law. And millions of Americans—like people the world over—seem to believe that a vague entity identified as "they" controls everything. "They're raising prices again. They're too soft on criminals. They're getting us into another war."

Disputes about the nature of the U.S. power structure extend into expert cir-

cles. Some sociologists and political scientists hold that America has an oligarchical, even élitist, system, with power—be it at the local, state or national level—firmly in the grasp of a relative few. According to this theory, most of the important decisions about public policy are made by the élite, and only the details are worked out in open debate. Other scholars of society and politics take a pluralist view, saying that the system truly does accommodate the multiplicity of wide-ranging interest groups, that it responds to shifting coalitions as they come together, achieve their purposes and then dissolve once again.

The majority of Americans would probably say that the pluralist version

comes closer to the truth, although élites certainly are part of the power structure of the United States. In many a small community, leading citizens gather in the local coffee shop to thrash out various issues privately before they attend a meeting in their official roles as members of the school board or city council to vote publicly on those same issues. Similarly, persons of substance in larger cities frequently find it more convenient, and more rewarding, to impart their views quietly to a mayor or governor, congressional representative or newspaper publisher while lunching at an exclusive club—such as the Pacific Union in San Francisco, the Somerset in Boston, or the Century in New York—than to declare their aims

116

to the public in an open forum.

But because the electorate can always use its votes to "turn the rascals out", in the words of an old American reformist battle cry, no élite can long maintain control of a city or state unless the government is satisfying the people. Sometimes the people are content as long as government is honest or at least has the appearance of honesty. In other instances, they appear to care less about honesty in government than about whether that government serves them in direct, tangible ways.

Such was long the case in Chicago, where the most important élite was the powerful Democratic Party machine that ran the city and rewarded those who brought in the votes with lucrative patronage jobs. Honesty in political matters was never Chicago's strong point. Party workers have been known to vote tombstones—that is, to assist their candidates into office by casting ballots in the names of citizens who were in fact dead. But as long as the machine dispensed government jobs and contracts to faithful supporters and helped citizens to deal with bureaucracy, it maintained tight control of the city. "Over at my headquarters," one longtime Chicago city council member explained to a reporter, "I've got lawyers, corporation counsel, an administrative assistant. You've got a legal matter? We turn it over to the lawyers. Free of charge. You've got a state matter? We've got a state representative in my organization. You've got a county matter? We've got a county commissioner. It doesn't matter what comes up. We give service."

Apparently the machine did not give enough service to a growing number of black voters, who in 1983 helped to elect Chicago's first black mayor. He

too was a Democrat, but the interests of his supporters did not mesh with those of the old machine, which had managed to retain a majority in the city council. The ensuing power struggle within the municipal government made it clear that Chicago politics would never be the same again, and that the old bosses would at the very least have to share their control of the city, if not yield it altogether.

At the national level, of course, the system is more complex. Many more interest groups are in contention; their leverage is greater and is usually applied with more sophistication; the stakes for which they compete are much higher. But the differences are matters of degree; the power structure of the U.S. as a whole is analogous to the system at state and local levels. The nation has, for instance, a power élite that in principle is not all that different from a small town's leading citizens gathering at the coffee shop.

A 1970 study of public and private positions of national authority revealed some surprising statistics. Barely 4,000 people in 5,400 key decision-making positions (some individuals filled more than one role) collectively controlled half the country's industrial assets, half its banking wealth, about half the wealth of private universities and foundations, and half the nation's transportation, communications and utilities. This handful of people (less than two thousandths of 1 per cent of the population) also ran the big television networks, newspaper chains and news agencies, the most important Washington and New York law firms, and the country's major cultural and civic organizations. And they held all the top jobs in the federal government—military as well as civilian.

While this seems to be an incredible concentration of power, the pluralists' argument is that these people failed to constitute a true élite, in the sense that they were not closely associated in a tight clique of common background and common aims. The American system certainly does allow for more vertical mobility than most other societies, and some of the people in top posts—especially those in military roles—rose from simple origins. Nonetheless, according to the criteria employed by Thomas R. Dye, the sociologist who carried out the 1970 study, fully 90 per cent of the 4,000 were born into America's social and economic upper and upper-middle classes—classes that accounted for only 22 per cent of the nation's total population.

Moreover, quite a few of those 4,000 were personally acquainted with one another. They had met through their work, or through ultraselective social organizations such as California's Bohemian Club *(page 12)* or through such influential policy-planning groups as

117

AN ENDURING PLAN OF GOVERNMENT

"The Constitution of the United States was made not merely for the generation that then existed," said 19th-century American statesman Henry Clay, "but for posterity—unlimited, undefined, endless, perpetual posterity." The genius of the Founding Fathers was to set out a plan incorporating an array of checks and balances. Powers were distributed among three branches of government—the executive, legislative and judicial.

The president, as chief executive, is the most powerful individual in government. He can veto legislation passed by the Congress and initiate legislation of his own. He is commander-in-chief of the armed forces and head of his political party. The president appoints his Cabinet but he must get the Senate's approval of his appointments. He also appoints the heads of numerous governmental agencies.

The two houses of Congress, the Senate and the House of Representatives, restrain the president's power. They initiate legislation of their own, act on or vote down presidential proposals, and can overturn a presidential veto on a bill if two thirds of the members of both houses agree. Senators are elected every six years, two from each state, while representatives are voted in for two-year terms from 435 congressional districts. By establishing two houses in Congress, the framers of the Constitution guaranteed that no single group would make the laws.

The Supreme Court can declare invalid any legislation or congressional or presidential decisions deemed incompatible with the Constitution. The nine justices of the Court are appointed by the president—with the approval of the Senate—and they have tenure for life.

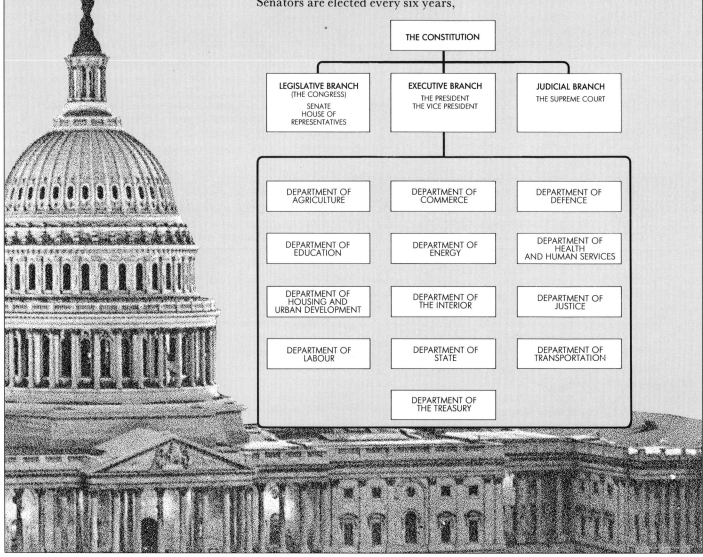

THE CONSTITUTION

LEGISLATIVE BRANCH
(THE CONGRESS)
SENATE
HOUSE OF REPRESENTATIVES

EXECUTIVE BRANCH
THE PRESIDENT
THE VICE PRESIDENT

JUDICIAL BRANCH
THE SUPREME COURT

DEPARTMENT OF AGRICULTURE

DEPARTMENT OF COMMERCE

DEPARTMENT OF DEFENCE

DEPARTMENT OF EDUCATION

DEPARTMENT OF ENERGY

DEPARTMENT OF HEALTH AND HUMAN SERVICES

DEPARTMENT OF HOUSING AND URBAN DEVELOPMENT

DEPARTMENT OF THE INTERIOR

DEPARTMENT OF JUSTICE

DEPARTMENT OF LABOUR

DEPARTMENT OF STATE

DEPARTMENT OF TRANSPORTATION

DEPARTMENT OF THE TREASURY

the Council on Foreign Relations, the Business Council and the Committee for Economic Development, which devote private money and effort to find solutions to public problems.

Eminence has its own rewards, and those who have made it to the top find it easy to circulate in the company of other "movers and shakers"—the achievers of America. Their inter-relationships can be glimpsed by taking note of just a few of the men who were members of both the Council on Foreign Relations and New York's Century Club during the late 1960s. Among a bevy of corporate chiefs, leading bankers and top-flight lawyers were editors of *Time, Newsweek* and *The New York Times*, multimillionaires John D. Rockefeller III and his brothers Nelson and David, perennial presidential adviser Henry Kissinger, prominent newspaper columnists Walter Lippmann and James Reston, then-Secretary of State Dean Rusk, a deputy secretary of defence, the president of the CBS broadcasting network and the chairman of the Ford Foundation.

Viewed from another perspective, however, the élite can appear much less formidable. In the first place, power in the U.S. is probably more widely dispersed than in many other major nations. It is likely, for instance, that the equivalent of the power exercised by those 4,000 Americans is concentrated in the hands of a few dozen individuals in a country like the Soviet Union.

Furthermore, the composition of the U.S. élite is constantly shifting as the mighty rise and fall, retire or die, and as voters oust one of the two major political parties from governmental office and replace it with the other.

In fact, the élite discerned by sociologist Dye in his 1970 study would have

a different complexion if examined little more than a decade later. In 1970 a loose-knit coalition of Democratic and Republican politicians, bankers, lawyers, industrialists and media people—tagged "the Eastern liberal establishment" because of its members' political philosophies and that most of them worked from power bases in north-eastern United States—was a loud and influential voice of American political life. But in later years it lost much influence to challengers that Dye labelled the "Sun Belt cowboys", political conservatives from the West and South, newly rich in oil, aerospace and property-boom money, and riding a tide of public resentment of high taxes and pervasive bureaucracy.

Another factor that restricts the power of any American national élite—and the power of the two major political parties themselves—is the complex and unwieldy law-making process. Under the parliamentary system used by most European nations, the party with a majority of legislators forms a government that can, generally speaking, put its programmes into effect with little difficulty. But under the American system, the party of the president might control only one—or perhaps neither—of the two law-making bodies of Congress, the Senate and the House of Representatives. In any case, both the Republican and Democratic parties encompass such wide ideological spectra that neither one can depend with any certainty on all of its senators and representatives agreeing on any given proposal.

Thus, as a bill (a proposed new law) makes its way through the labyrinth of committees and subcommittees in both houses, the contending legislators each give a little and get a little, lubricating

the process with compromise. "The oilcan is mightier than the sword," said the last Senator Everett Dirksen, a master at the game.

At every turn, legislators are subject to blandishments and pressures from outside forces—sometimes a lawmaker's home-state constituents, but more often some of the 6,000 lobbyists who work for special-interest groups such as corporations, ex-servicemen and women or farmers. Lobbyists do not always get what they want, but they are usually given a hearing because they take pains to cultivate legislators, doing favours for them and often helping to finance their election campaigns. Of the 25,000 or so bills introduced in Congress over a two-year period, as few as 700 may become law.

To steer a bill through this political obstacle course, a politician must employ clever strategies and win influential support at key points of decision. "Once begin the dance of legislation," said President Woodrow Wilson, "and you must struggle through its mazes as best you can to the breathless end—if any end there be." An example of what Wilson meant—and a revealing lesson in the realities of the American power structure—is the odyssey taken by first-term Senator Pete V. Domenici, a Republican from New Mexico, when he set out in February 1977 to secure a relatively minor piece of legislation: a law that would require users of inland waterways to help the federal government pay for the waterways' construction and maintenance.

Whereas transport firms paid tolls, licence fees and fuel taxes to help subsidize motorways—and railways built and maintained their own tracks—water-cargo carriers, which hauled 16 per cent of the nation's inland freight,

5

contributed not a penny towards the expense of dams, locks, dredging and general upkeep of the 40,000-kilometre waterway system. All of the work was done at public expense by the U.S. Army Corps of Engineers.

Domenici, who served on the Senate's Environment and Public Works Committee, considered the free use of waterways to be clearly inequitable—perhaps particularly so because he came from a state that had no barge lines and lots of railways. His interest in the question became charged with fervour one day during a hearing on the need to rebuild a large waterway facility in Illinois called Lock and Dam 26. He casually asked several witnesses, who included representatives of inland shipping companies, whether the barge industry itself should not pay for the new construction. "Some of those barge guys jumped right out of their skins when I brought it up," he later recalled. Indeed, one of them shouted angrily at Domenici: "You don't have any waterways in New Mexico. What business is it of yours?"

"Mister," replied Domenici, his temper igniting, "you're going to find out what business it is of mine." He then turned to two aides and snapped, "Get me a user-charge bill."

The aides drafted legislation for a system of waterway user fees. But similar bills had been proposed before, and all had collapsed under pressure from barge interests and their powerful advocates in Congress, who liked the cheap shipping rates that farmers and manufacturers in their home states enjoyed from the barge lines. Rather than confront the opposition head on, Domenici tried a congressional tactic known as piggy-backing. He attached his proposal to a piece of legislation

PLAYGROUND OF THE POWERFUL

What has been called "the greatest men's party on earth" takes place every July at a California campsite called Bohemian Grove, located in a 1,100-hectare redwood forest 105 kilometres north of San Francisco. The party consists of a huge two-week camp-out attended by more than 2,000 men (and men only).

It is a remarkable gathering largely because these 2,000 include many of the richest and most powerful individuals in America, from the presidents of the nation's largest corporations and banks to presidents of the United States.

The Grove and its camp buildings are owned by San Francisco's Bohemian Club, founded in 1872 as a refuge for writers, actors and other "bohemians" of the arts. The club was soon taken over, however, by the city's merchants and moneymen, and it has been a bastion of the well-to-do ever since.

The July camp sessions, begun in 1878, were once simply informal get-togethers (below), but soon became known (though not widely known) as meetings of the mighty.

Today, a majority of the club's members remain Californians, but men from most of the other 49 states also hold coveted memberships. President Herbert Hoover, Richard Nixon and Ronald Reagan have belonged to the club, as have many secretaries of state, commerce and defence. Although the ostensible purpose is relaxation, two weeks of proximity helps to knit together these members of the power élite. The Grove has long been, as one journalist put it, "a major showcase", where the leaders in business and politics, in education and the arts "can come to examine each other"—and where they can make many momentous decisions about the future of the nation.

Club members relax at Bohemian Grove in 1907, 29 years after the first outing.

120

that barge owners eagerly supported: a bill to spend $400 million to rebuild Lock and Dam 26.

Railway lobbyists, of course, were delighted with Domenici's proposal. So were environmentalists, who had long been unhappy that barge traffic and excessive construction of dams and locks destroyed wildlife habitats, reduced the recreational use of rivers and polluted public waters. But that support was offset by Domenici's potential antagonists, among them such powerful river-state senators as Louisiana's Russell B. Long, chairman of the Finance Committee, Mississippi's John C. Stennis, head of the Armed Forces Committee, and the state of Washington's Warren G. Magnuson, steward of the Commerce Committee.

Domenici knew his bill would never reach the Senate floor for a vote if he launched it solely in one of the committees ruled by these user-fee opponents. But because it would be impolitic to try to hurdle all of them at the outset, Domenici had the bill sent, simultaneously, to the Commerce Committee and to his own Public Works Committee. A favourable recommendation from only one committee would bring the bill to the Senate floor for debate.

The Republican Senator got some help from Democratic President Jimmy Carter's administration when the Transportation Secretary Brock Adams testified at a hearing on the proposal. "It is simply not just," he declared, "that profit-making businesses should have this much of their costs met by the American taxpayer." Domenici also got an unexpected boost from Illinois's Republican Senator Charles H. Percy, who risked antagonizing his own constituents by declaring, "I am absolutely convinced, and have

told the barge owners this, the free ride is over. To keep up these waterways, the user must pay for the service." Buoyed by this support, Domenici steered the combined Lock 26 and user-fee bill to a 14-1 endorsement by the full committee. This was in May of 1977.

With the bill headed for a debate on the Senate floor, Domenici managed to enlist more help from President Carter, who made it known that he would "veto any bill authorizing construction of a new Lock and Dam 26 which does not also contain a provision for waterway user charges".

A preliminary head count in the Senate indicated a close vote with about 40 senators lined up on each side and 20 uncommitted. It was now June, and lobbyists went to work on the uncommitted. J.D. Feeney, the genial ("Call me Joe") general counsel of the Western Railroads Association, captained the lobbying team on Domenici's side, while cocky St. Louis B. Susman, a well-connected member of the Democratic National Committee, became the chief persuader for the barge owners. Each side had put together a campaign fund of about $500,000, mainly from corporate contributions.

While the barge interests had financed their lobbyists openly, the pro-Domenici forces had been faced by a special problem that required a delicate solution. Although they could count on the railways for support, they could ill-afford to have them as allies: the railways were the barge industry's competition, and their motives bound to be regarded as suspect. So the pro-Domenici forces tried another tack. They turned to the environmentalists, who they knew were opposed to the barge interests, and arranged for the railways to give them financial aid. The

environmentalists, however, had reservations. "If you ever wanted to see a bunch of people who were skittish about dealing with railroads," chortled Joe Feeney, "it was those bearded environmentalists. Hell, some of those guys had sued us a few times."

Feeney arranged a bit of dubious but time-honoured Washington hanky-panky: he set up what is called a laundry, a bank account in the name of a bogus organization. The name of the organization was the Council for a Sound Waterway Policy, and the address on its letterhead was a vacant railway office. Through it, Feeney pumped up to $5,000 a month to environmental groups, thus enabling them to lobby effectively on behalf of the bill.

Probably the most bizarre aspect of the lobbying campaign's finances was the role of United States Steel; it actually managed to lobby on both sides of the question. United States Steel's wholly owned subsidiary, the Elgin, Joliet and Eastern Railroad, gave several thousand dollars to support the user-fee proposal, while another United States Steel satrapy, the Ohio Barge Line, Inc., donated similar funds to try to defeat the measure.

The final days before the June vote provided a textbook display of behind-the-scenes activity in Congress. Domenici tried to nail down the votes of three Western Republicans for his bill, but he learnt that Senator Stennis had captured their allegiance by threatening to oppose funding for an irrigation project they wanted for their states. President Carter won the support of West Virginia's Senator Jennings Randolph by promising to campaign for him. And Russell Long guaranteed favourable Finance Committee action on a tax bill backed by a Delaware Re-

5

publican in return for that Senator's vote against the user fee.

When Long learnt that two pro-user-fee senators were away on business, he tried a tough-minded ploy, calling for a vote on June 22. To the astonishment of Senate veterans, Domenici's bill was passed, 71 votes to 20. "You'll never guess what happened," a reporter was heard yelling into a telephone. "Pete Domenici went head to head with Russell Long, and Domenici won!"

The victory was short-lived. The bill contained a serious flaw: according to the Constitution, all revenue-raising laws must originate in the House of Representatives. Domenici had hoped his proposal would be interpreted as a regulatory measure, rather than a revenue bill. But the chairman of the House Ways and Means Committee, Oregon's Al Ullman, tersely informed the Senate that it had violated the Constitution. The Domenici bill was stuck.

At this critical point, the Democratic administration gave more help to the Republican Senator. It enlisted the aid of Thomas P. "Tip" O'Neill Jr., who—as leader of the Democratic majority in the lower legislative body—was Speaker of the House. A master with the oilcan, the crafty, imposing, white-haired Boston Irishman convinced leading members of Congress that the bill ought to be introduced as a brand-new measure in the House. But the representatives added a provision that dismayed Domenici: instead of a direct user fee, revenues would come from a tax on barge diesel fuel. And the tax would be only four to six cents per gallon, low enough for barge owners to accept. On October 13, the House passed the measure, 331 to 70.

The bill returned to the Senate, where Domenici sought to restore his principle of payments directly related to use. The bargemen, who had been amenable to compromise in the House, talked tough again. They wanted the bill stopped. That was too much for Russell Long, whose credo as a senator was negotiation and accommodation.

"I'm likely to get a little perturbed with these fellows," he remarked. "There comes a time when you have to get realistic and give an inch or two. That's how legislating works."

Long and Domenici, fearing they might lose a straight vote on the Senate floor, tried through intermediaries to reach a compromise. But the effort was unsuccessful. "They're like a pair of sumo wrestlers," said an observer. "They dance around throwing salt in the air, but they're afraid to get in the ring." Domenici finally struck a bargain with another opponent of his proposal, Illinois Democrat Adlai E. Stevenson. They drafted a measure to include the diesel tax and a separate, modest-sized user fee. President Carter announced that the compromise was the minimum he would accept.

But when the revised bill reached the Senate floor in May 1978, the farm lobby, concerned that the user fee would increase farmers' freight rates, joined the barge interests in opposing it, and some farm-state senators who had been supporters became foes. Several other senators, because they were up for re-election in 1978, could no longer afford to oppose the rivermen in their home states. This time the Senate voted Domenici's bill down, 47 to 43, accepting instead the diesel-tax measure passed by the House. Hearing the news, President Carter promised to veto the bill if it reached his desk.

Now nobody had anything to show for all the months of hard, abrasive work. The barge industry was getting no new Lock and Dam 26; Domenici's user-fee principle was out the window; the President appeared in an unpopular negative position; and the river-state legislators had gained nothing for the folks back home. Suddenly both camps seemed ready for serious and sustained negotiations.

Together they came up with a well-oiled compromise: a new Inland Waterways Trust Fund would be created by the bill. The trust would receive the diesel-tax monies (with the tax rate now raised to 10 cents a gallon), and the revenue would be entirely devoted to maintaining the waterways. And, of course, the package featured a rebuilt Lock and Dam 26.

Long, Domenici and Carter all endorsed the amended measure. By the time the much-repaired bill was ready for a vote on October 6, however, only eight days remained in the 1978 congressional session, and there was no telling how the measure might fare if it was held over till the next Congress. Urgent action by a master of parliamentary tactics was required. Russell Long agreed to provide it. "We just have to find a vehicle, and that's no problem," he said. "I've always got a few little bills back in the office."

What Long meant was that he would attach the waterways measure to some minor bill that had already passed the House and was resting in his Senate office, awaiting a propitious moment. When the "little bill" went to the Senate floor, the real issue coud be attached to it as an amendment. Senator Long rooted out a measure that authorized certain charitable organizations to run tax-free bingo games. The odd combination of a bingo measure and the waterways legislation quickly came

A HOUSE FOR ALL THE PEOPLE

During a celebration of the national game, children play baseball on the South Lawn.

Thomas Jefferson, the first President to spend a full term living in the White House, helped to set the tone for that handsome mansion, as he did for many other American institutions. Arranging a dinner party during his 1801–1809 tenure in office, he invited several important officials—and then he added his butcher's name to the guest list.

History fails to record whether any subsequent presidents have invited their suppliers of chops and roasts to dine. But the executive mansion has remained what President Franklin D. Roosevelt called it, "a house owned by all the American people". A number of the rooms are open to the public five days each week; in recent years about 1.5 million visitors have toured the mansion annually, or have attended such yearly events as the egg-rolling for children at Easter and the spring garden tour. And there are many other informal events, even including games on the lawn *(above)*. It seems safe to say that in no other nation is the chief executive's residence so available to the American population.

Not all of the White House's 132 rooms are, of course, open to the public. Twenty-five rooms on the second and third floors provide private living quarters for the presidential family. These include a small kitchen and dining room. For formal entertaining of foreign heads of state and other dignitaries there are two principal rooms, the State Dining Room and the East Room.

This large establishment requires more than 85 full-time employees, from cooks to electricians to a cleaning staff (which uses 1,350 kilograms of detergent each year), plus 17 gardeners to care for the 7 hectares of grounds. The kitchen where large banquets are prepared has four full-time chefs. The budget for official entertaining, voted by Congress, exceeds $200,000 a year. The number of guests attending White House functions can exceed 75,000 annually.

But even the most august affairs are relatively modest. The State Dining Room seats a maximum of 140. Even the name of the building reflects a certain modesty. It is called the "White House" for a quite mundane reason. British troops set fire to the building during the War of 1812; it has been painted white ever since in order to hide the ugly burn marks on the stone wall.

to the floor, and the Senate passed it by a unanimous voice vote.

Now the jerry-built measure had to get through the House of Representatives, since it was no longer the mere bingo bill previously passed by that body. O'Neill, who had been brought into Long's plan, was ready. Under a special provision known as suspension, he brought the bill directly on to the floor for a fast vote—with no stops in committees along the way. When the tally was taken—a year and seven months after the New Mexico Senator had introduced his original bill and only 26 hours before Congress was scheduled to adjourn—Pete Domenici had won at last, 287 to 123.

Thus are most laws in Washington created, by canny legislators who can get the business accomplished. But occasionally the system must respond to an anguished cry for justice or progress from the nation as a whole, or from a large section of the population. At such times the needed legislation may be fashioned and driven into being by political adroitness outside the formal lawmaking process as well as inside it. That was the case in the 1960s, when a black preacher named Martin Luther King Jr. led a drive to secure full voting rights for America's blacks.

In many parts of the South, literacy tests, poll taxes and physical intimidation had been used to keep blacks away from the ballot boxes and politically powerless. For example, the literacy test for voter registration in Alabama's Dallas County—given only twice a month—required that an applicant write from dictation a part of the Constitution and answer eight questions on the governmental process. Although the population of Alabama was almost 60 per cent black, 9,542 local whites

made it on to the country's voting rolls while only 335 blacks qualified.

At that pace, protested King, who had been organizing demonstrations for racial equality since the 1950s, "it would take 103 years to register the adult Negroes". And those blacks who tried to assert their right to vote were likely to be manhandled by Dallas County Sheriff Jim Clark, who authorized his deputies to use electric cattle prods to deter demonstrators.

King chose the town of Selma, the Dallas County seat, as the crucible for forging a new law to end voter discrimination once and for all. His strategy was to dramatize the plight of the Southern blacks through confrontations between peaceable marchers and hot-tempered, armed local police. King believed that national press coverage of attacks on his people would arouse the conscience of the nation.

In January 1965, he led 400 blacks in the first of several marches to the Dallas County courthouse in Selma. Events developed as King had foreseen. A photograph showing Sheriff Clark roughing up a woman protestor appeared in Northern newspapers. A few days later, Clark clubbed another woman while two other officers held her down. King was jailed for violating a town ordinance against unauthorized parades, and 500 protesting school-children also were locked up. New York Senator Jacob K. Javits called the arrests "shocking", and a group of liberal congress members made plans to visit Selma. "There are more Negroes in jail with me," King wrote, "than there are on the voting rolls."

President Lyndon B. Johnson made it known that he was ready for quick and serious talks with King about future legislation in order to end voting discrimination. The black leader was granted bail, and a couple of days later he flew to Washington for a meeting with President Johnson. King said he favoured a voting rights bill that would cover both state and federal elections, eliminate literacy tests and empower federal officials to enforce fair registration procedures. Johnson's aides began drawing up just such a bill, and King returned to the South to keep the pres-

Linking arms with other civil rights leaders, the Reverend Martin Luther King Jr. (second from right) marches in Memphis, Tennessee, to demonstrate for equal rights, a week before his assassination in April 1968.

sure up, telling his followers, "We are going to bring a voting bill into being in the streets of Selma."

The struggle was getting bloody. On February 18, an Alabama state trooper shot and mortally wounded 26-year-old protestor Jimmy Lee Jackson while he walked with other blacks in a demonstration in the adjacent county. On March 7, King's deputy Hosea Williams was leading some 525 protestors across a Selma bridge on the start of an 86-kilometre-hike to the state capital of Montgomery when about 50 state policemen and several local officers, some on horseback, charged into the crowd in a flying wedge, tossing tear gas and flailing the blacks with clubs and whips. "The wedge moved with such force that it seemed almost to pass over the waiting column instead of through it," a journalist reported.

Several protestors lay wounded while policemen chased other demonstrators through the streets of Selma. Many blacks suffered broken ribs, head gashes and other injuries. That evening, viewers all across the nation saw the brutal assault on television newscasts. Two days later, racist thugs beat up and mortally injured a white minister named James Reeb, who had travelled south from Boston to offer his moral support to the protest.

Hundreds of outraged people from all over the U.S.—students, clergymen, housewives—flocked to Selma to enlist in King's army. While pickets demanding action staged a sit-in at the White House in Washington, administration lawyers hurried to finish a draft bill. At the end of the week President Johnson told a joint session of Congress that the legislation was ready. "Their cause must be our cause too," he said of King's legions. "It is all of us who must overcome the crippling legacy of bigotry and injustice."

More and more aroused Americans journeyed to Alabama to join the movement. Alabama Governor George C. Wallace, who had tried to stop the demonstrations, telegraphed the President that the state lacked the means to protect marchers or sympathetic bystanders. That was too much for Lyndon Johnson. He federalized the Alabama National Guard, putting that state militia's officers under his orders to prevent further violence.

Meanwhile, the voting rights bill had irresistible support. The President, leaders of both parties, the national press, churches and labour unions joined the black civil rights leaders in advocating prompt enactment. The bill that arrived in the Senate from the President acquired sponsorship by a bi-partisan coalition of 66 senators.

During the debate a few Southern senators challenged the measure, arguing that states had the right to set their own voting standards. But after offering a desultory flurry of amendments, opponents of the bill fell back, demoralized. "I assume the die is cast," sighed Georgia's Senator Richard Russell.

In Alabama, some 25,000 people, black and white, had descended on Montgomery, where they were protected by the National Guard. "We are on the move now," King told them. "We are moving to the land of freedom." That night, a white woman from Detroit, Viola Liuzzo, was murdered in a Ku Klux Klan ambush as she was travelling in a car to Montgomery. She was the last casualty in the crusade for a law to guarantee equality at the polls.

The following week, the U.S. Senate passed the Voting Rights Act of 1965 by a stunning majority of 77 to 19. The bill then stalled in the House for several weeks, because of the recalcitrance of Rules Committee Chairman Howard Smith of Virginia. He called the new measure unconstitutional, asserting that it was "dripping in venom" and that it would allow the U.S. Attorney General "almost unlimited power to investigate, to prosecute and to try and convict sovereign states."

But many of his own Southern colleagues thought differently about the bill. Louisiana's Hale Boggs said in a speech to the House, "I love my state. I love the South. I support this bill because I believe the fundamental right to vote must be a part of this great experiment in human progress under freedom which is America." The House finally passed the bill by an overwhelming vote of 333 to 85.

When President Johnson signed the act into law on August 6, he declared that "the last of the legal barriers" to racial equality had come down. Before the end of the month, 27,385 blacks had been registered as voters by the federal examiners in the counties of Alabama, Louisiana and Mississippi.

In the ensuing decade and beyond, the law was to alter the contours of Southern politics, as blacks in large numbers exercised their franchise for the first time. President Johnson called the Voting Rights Act "one of the most monumental laws in the history of American freedom". He could rightly have added that the story of the law's creation was itself a monument—a monument to a system that is often clumsy, that sometimes evokes justifiable cynicism by favouring the powerful, but that has proved its ability, when pressed, to serve democratically the needs of all the people.

REDEFINING WOMEN'S ROLES

The smiling police officer on the right represents a dramatic change in American life: Beth Atkins of the Chicago Police Department is one of the more than 45 million women in the United States now working. In the early 1960s, only 40 per cent of the female population between the ages of 20 and 34 held jobs outside the home. Today, the proportion is two thirds, and it is estimated that 95 per cent of American women aged 25 to 34 will be working by 1995. Moreover, women are turning away from the "pink collar" clerical and secretarial jobs they have traditionally held in great numbers and they are joining the ranks of doctors, lawyers, airline pilots and other professions once almost exclusively held by men.

What this social revolution means in domestic terms can be seen in the daily routine of Chicago police officers Beth and Mike Atkins and their daughters, Amy, 11, and Eileen, nine. The Atkinses are fortunate because Mike, who has been a detective on the police force for more than a decade, can select his work shift so as to be home while Beth is on patrol. Amy and Eileen have become more independent and like having more of each parent's time. Combined wages give the family money to spend on weekly family outings.

The Atkinses have discovered that they must all be more considerate of one another. Once, after tidying up the house and going to work, Beth returned to find objects and clothes scattered about. There was a polite but strained family conference, and since then Mike and the girls have taken responsibility for cleaning up whatever mess they create. Mike, in agreeing to share some of the household chores, has begun to do the ironing.

Amused by an exchange heard on her radio, Chicago police officer Beth Atkins shares the remark with her training officer, Jack Murphy. As a recruit, she will patrol with a training officer for three months.

Beth runs her daily 9 kilometres through the neighbourhood, accompanied by Amy on her bicycle. Although her most arduous previous exercise was shopping, Beth is now so fit that she has been named top female athlete in her class of recruits.

Rushing off to work at 7.20 a.m., Beth gives her husband a quick kiss. She has made breakfast for him and daughters Eileen (*left*) and Amy. Mike will drive the girls to school.

Lined up at the lockers with fellow recruits, Beth joins the discussion after a Police Academy class on defence tactics.

On patrol in Chicago's North Side, Jack Murphy and Beth Atkins write up a disturbance-of-the-peace report *(above)*. Later, Beth helps a victim of attempted robbery *(above, right)*, and keeps her sense of humour when a street vendor *(right)* responds to her request to move on with a cajoling, "You sure are pretty."

Beth practises regularly in the academy firing range. A crack shot, she ranked in the top 10 per cent of her class.

Mike watches television while he does the ironing, a chore that convention would prevent men in many other countries from taking on.

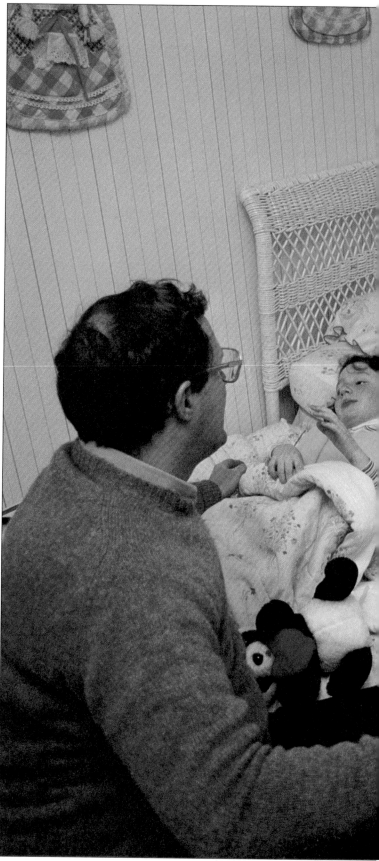

Making the most of their time with their daughters, Mike and Beth say an affectionate goodnight to Eileen *(left)* and Amy. As part of a regular ritual, all four pray together before the girls' lights are turned off.

Pillared porticos, lush lawns and
outdoor swimming pools proclaim
the prosperity of those who have
made it in the coal-mining town of
Pikeville, Kentucky. "We're not the
idle rich," says one resident of this
plush subdivision. "We're working
wealthy, not investor wealthy."

THE AMERICAN DREAM

A jetliner bearing the Great Seal of the United States touched down at West Berlin's Tempelhof Airport and rolled to a stop. On to the red-carpeted steps appeared W. Michael Blumenthal, U.S. Secretary of the Treasury, on a government mission. A cluster of dignitaries moved forward to greet him, and to walk him past a military guard of honour to a waiting limousine.

Someone handed Blumenthal a local morning paper. On the front page was his picture, with a biographical sketch pointing out that the Secretary, in making this visit to Berlin in February 1978, was returning to his native city. It was true: a member of the U.S. Cabinet, and an American citizen for most of his adult life, Michael Blumenthal was by birth a Berliner, the son of a Jewish shopkeeper. "I thought it was coming full circle," he said, "that the people who had kicked me out now would put my picture on the front page and call me proudly a 'Berliner'." And as he read through the story, his mind drifted back to the day, nearly 40 years earlier, when he and his family had fled Nazi Germany, and to the events that had carried him around the world to America—and to the highest levels of personal achievement. It was a classic tale of an immigrant who made good, and represented in clearest outline what the world has come to think of as the American Dream.

The Blumenthals had left Germany in 1938, when Michael was 12. Their destination was Shanghai, then an open city where no special papers were required. There, Michael's parents scrounged a living selling clothing while Michael attended a local British school. In 1942 the Japanese took over the city and herded them into a ghetto with the rest of Shanghai's refugees.

Release came in 1945, with the arrival of U.S. forces. The American soldiers, Blumenthal remembered, were "different from other people I knew—healthier, athletic, cleaner. They seemed more fun-loving, more joyful. And richer. Even the privates had what appeared to be a lot of money." But there was another difference that impressed him more. They were optimistic: "Most of them felt they had something going for them, and they could do what they wanted.

"I had lived in an environment, ever since I was old enough to realize what was going on, in which there were many, many restrictions placed on my ability to do the things I wanted to do," he recalled. Those restrictions "had nothing to do with me or with what I was capable of doing or willing to do. They had more to do with what my surname was, who my parents were, whether I had the right kind of passport, whether I was accepted in the right kind of school or the right kind of club, or whether I belonged to this group or that." The Americans he saw ignored such irrelevancies. "The average GI really exhibited the sense that,

6

while he might be a corporal and some-one else was a lieutenant or captain, he was as good as that person, even though one had a higher rank or was in a different category."

His reaction was clear. "I wanted to be like them. And I felt I could compete and do as well as they could."

Blumenthal eventually wangled a visa for the United States, stamped and signed on the back by the U.S. vice-consul. He and his sister sailed for San Francisco in September 1947 aboard a converted troopship. Within five days of landing, both of them had found jobs, she as a secretary, he as an advertising clerk earning $40 a week.

It did not take Blumenthal long to discover that the fastest journey up the career ladder in America is through education. He enrolled in a junior college, took a second job as a lift operator at St. Francis Hospital, and eventually transferred to the University of California at Berkeley, from which he graduated in 1951.

From then on, the path was clear. It carried the future Treasury Secretary to a doctorate from Princeton and the vice-presidency of a small company. In 1960 there was a telephone call from the White House. "We're looking for people with some business experience and some international economics background," said a presidential aide. "How would you like to work for the government?" In two months he was in Washington as a deputy assistant secretary at the State Department.

On his first day in office, he hunted through the Department telephone directory for the name of the vice-consul who, 14 years earlier, had signed his visa. "He had been a demi-god to me," Blumenthal remembered, "but there was, of course, no reason why he should remember me. He had given visas to thousands of people." So the man was understandably mystified by a call from a high official.

"Yes, sir, what can I do for you?"

"Well, I'd like to have lunch with you," said Blumenthal.

"Do I know you?"

"I'll explain it all when I see you."

The two men met in the Secretaries' dining room, which was reserved for

A river of runners engulfs six lanes of motorway just after the start of the annual New York City Marathon. So popular has the race become among physical-fitness buffs that the number of runners has to be limited by a lottery to 16,000 each year.

officials of senior rank and thus represented something of a treat for Blumenthal's guest. Blumenthal pulled out his old Shanghai identity card, frayed and rumpled with time, and handed it across the table. The man examined it, turned it over, and on the back was the visa with his signature. "Well, I'll be damned," he said.

Since then, Blumenthal has moved onwards and upwards, from government to private business and back again. But that stroke of recognition in the State Department dining room remains perhaps his proudest memory, when he felt he had truly arrived.

This rags-to-riches scenario has been acted out so many times in so many different ways by so many people—from the first settlers to more recent arrivals like Blumenthal—that it has become the essence of the American Dream. Yet material success is only one of many American Dreams. They exist in hundreds of shapes and variations, and find their realization in unnumbered circumstances. All of them share a belief in unlimited opportunity: a firm conviction that with effort and luck, almost anyone can make their life what they want it to be. "If one advances confidently in the direction of his dreams," said philosopher Henry David Thoreau, "and endeavours to live the life which he has imagined, he will meet with a success unexpected in common hours."

Perhaps the highest of these dreams is good works. Americans are indoctrinated to help their fellows. If they are driven to acquire wealth, they are also driven to give it away once acquired. The Rockefellers and Fricks are famous philanthropists, but most humanitarianism is supported by people unknown outside their own communities; the average American gives away about 2 per cent of earned income. Between individual gifts and the gifts of the nation's tens of thousands of philanthropic foundations, the annual total of donations in the U.S. amounts to about $40 billion.

Material things do not figure at all in the dreams of many Americans. They seek to fulfil inner goals. Some follow their own visions of God; a recent count found 336,281 religious groups in the U.S. Others pursue the will-o'-the-wisp of constant change; for these restless, never-satisfied individuals the dream is always something new, something different. Americans move an average of 13 times during their lifetime (by contrast, Britons change residence eight times, Japanese five). They switch jobs about 10 times. In her book *Pathfinders*, journalist Gail Sheehy writes of a man who was, successively and usually successfully, a steelworker, soldier, financial researcher, investment adviser, stockbroker, ski instructor, teacher of the blind and mayor.

The lure of easy change can lead many to turn away from the mainstream of society, giving up city life for some simple rural existence, or—more dramatically—becoming hedonistic wanderers living hand to mouth in a land of plenty. Some seek to create a better social system by establishing utopian communities. America has always been a haven for utopias; the first, Plockhoy's Commonwealth, was founded by Dutch Mennonite Pieter Plockhoy in 1663 by the Delaware River, and new ones still appear.

All these dreams, some more admirable than others, depend on opportunity that is equal for all—the chance to "do what they wanted to do", in Blumenthal's words. America is the land of opportunity, according to the cliché. But in recent times this reality has been challenged. Blumenthal could be the exception, not the rule.

The doubts are justified. Not all the early settlers made it, and neither have all later arrivals or their descendants. Many of them returned to the Old World; others lie in unmarked paupers' graves. From 1908 to 1923, 50 out of every 100 immigrants who came to the U.S. from southern Italy, Russia and the Balkan countries returned to their homeland. Poverty, ethnic bigotry, a home environment different from that of the dominant culture (middle-class, Anglo-Saxon) may limit the chance to try for the dream. More than 30 million Americans now live below the poverty level. For members of racial minorities, the situation is the bleakest: the poverty rate among whites is 11 per cent, but for Hispanics it is 26.5 per cent; for blacks, 34.2 per cent.

The unemployment rate for minorities is also high: in 1982 fewer than two thirds of black men were employed, compared with about 75 per cent of whites. A disproportionate

Sporting shamrocks on their hats—and braces on their teeth—teenage girls celebrate St. Patrick's Day in Chicago. Similar festivities are held in other cities as well, wherever Irish-Americans are numerous.

6

number of black teenagers are out of work: in 1954 almost 55 per cent of them were employed; by 1982, only 20 per cent—one in five—were working.

And yet the American Dreams are alive and well. People do get an opportunity—many opportunities—to make their lives what they want them to be. The evidence is obvious for the dream of material success. Blumenthal, it turns out, is no exception:

William Black started with a shelled-nuts stand in the Times Square theatre district of New York City. At the time of his death he owned a city-wide chain of lunch counters pulling in more than $100 million a year.

Mo Siegel, a laid-back 20-year-old hippie, began combing the hills near his Colorado home for the ingredients of herbal teas; in six years his blends brought him his first million dollars.

Jennifer Steves, a Philadelphia social worker, began buying run-down Victorian town houses, sprucing them up, and using the refurbished dwellings as collateral to buy more houses. She soon owned 30 properties, and had a personal fortune of $2 million.

Steven Jobs and Stephen Wozniak, college dropouts barely out of their teens, built their first home computer in Jobs's parents' garage in Los Altos, California. Within five years, annual sales of their Apple computers had soared to $600 million, and the two founders were individually worth hundreds of millions of dollars.

Financial success stories are easy to find. By the 1980s, some 600,000 Americans were millionaires, and the number rises about 10 per cent a year.

The dream achieved can be seen in the sprawl of motorways and split-level suburbs, of beach resorts and holiday homes, of shopping malls and gourmet supermarkets, and in the statistics of national well-being. The U.S. standard of living was the highest among the industrial countries in 1980, as reported by the Organization for Economic Cooperation and Development. Of the 800 million households in the U.S., 64 per cent owned their own living quarters, 51 per cent had more than one vehicle, and 55 per cent had at least two TV sets. Almost 10 per cent of American workers ran their own businesses, and 54 per cent of all wage earners in 1982 held white-collar jobs. A carpenter or mechanic was paid about $18,000 a year, more than triple the average for manufacturing jobs in Greece or Taiwan.

The vitality of the success dream is perhaps best seen in the experience of the recent wave of immigrants from Asia and the Pacific. A few have made millions; many have found the solid middle-class comfort they hoped for.

Among the fastest climbers have been the Koreans, about 500,000, who arrived in the U.S. after 1968, when anti-Asian immigration quotas were eased. Their enterprise is visible in most major American cities. In New York City they number 100,000, and in 12 years have come to dominate the $500-million retail produce business, distributing two million tonnes of fruits and vegetables a year. They own three quarters of the 1,200 or so greengrocers in the metropolitan area.

Young Jun Kwon is typical of the Koreans who have made it in this back-breaking and stressful work. In 1973, after a stint in the Korean Army, he pulled up stakes and moved to New York to join his sister and brother-in-law. He got work as a janitor in a wire and cable company, and soon advanced to foreman. Then he married,

STRUGGLE FOR A BETTER LIFE

Before the Pilgrims arrived on the rocky shore of Massachusetts in 1620, there already were Europeans living in what would eventually become the United States. These settlers were the Spaniards of Florida and the South-west.

Today, Hispanics, such as tractor operator Isauro Rios *(right)*, are the country's fastest-growing minority. By official count, they number 14.6 million. Their ranks are continually swelled by immigrants arriving legally, at the rate of 250,000 a year, from the Caribbean and from Central and South America. Most of these are Mexicans, Puerto Ricans and Cubans. Many more Hispanics are entering the country illegally. The U.S. Bureau of the Census estimates that 1.4 million of the Hispanics counted in the 1980 census had entered the country without proper immigration papers. At any particular time, there may be 480,000 to 1.22 million Mexican "illegals" working in the United States, their numbers rising and falling with the seasonal availability of jobs in agriculture.

If the Hispanic-American population continues to increase at its present rate, Hispanics will outnumber U.S. blacks within the next decade, to become the country's largest minority. Already 25 cities have Hispanic communities of 50,000 or more. Los Angeles County alone counts more than 2.5 million Hispanics amongst its 7.9 million people.

The Hispanic groups are as different from one another as are their countries of origin or the U.S. locales in which most of them settle—Cubans in Florida, Puerto

Tractor operator Isauro Rios stands between his one-room plywood home and a pile of breeze blocks for the four-room house he is building.

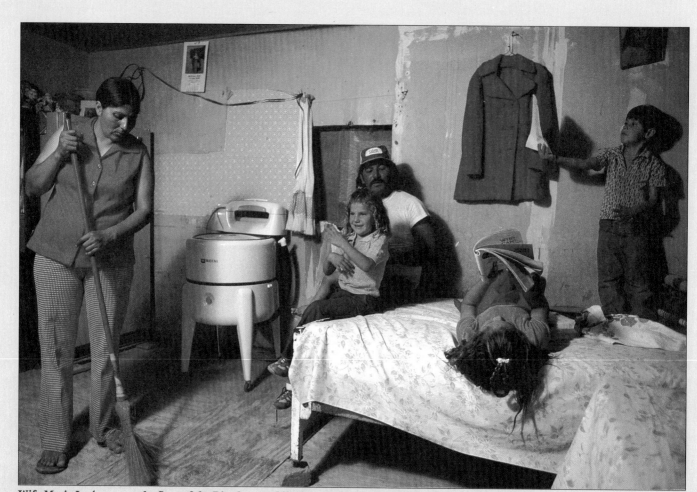

Wife Maria Jesús sweeps the floor of the Rios house while Isauro relaxes with children Maria Oneida *(left)*, Wencelada and Juan Carlos.

Ricans in New York, Mexicans in the West and South-west. What they have most in common is a proud determination to enter the American mainstream despite the political, economic and social barriers that most of them constantly encounter. And unlike many of the immigrants who preceded them, they wish to do so without having their own identities and culture subsumed as they become Americans. Some are insisting that Spanish, not English, be taught as a first language in the public schools their children attend.

Isauro Rios is a stocky, horny-handed farm labourer who lives and works just across the Rio Grande from the land of his Mexican ancestors. His way of life

exemplifies many of the difficulties and, in even greater measure, the determination of his fellow Hispanics.

Rios has some advantages over bewildered newcomers to the United States, and particularly over the apprehensive illegals, who throng the great metropolitan centres. American-born and bilingual, he was already in place, so to speak, before the great waves of Hispanic immigration actually began. But he happens to live and work in one of the Promised Land's least promising locations.

Home for Isauro is the tiny community of La Puerta in Starr County, down at the bottom of Texas and near the bottom of the U.S. economy. The county's population of 27,000 is 97 per cent

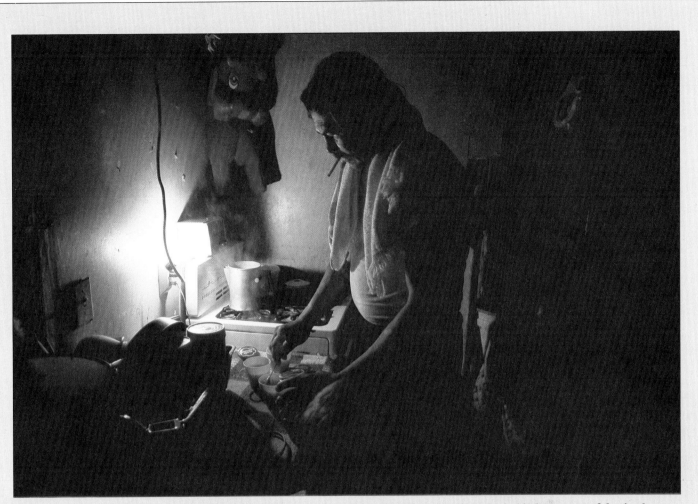

A work day for Isauro begins at 6 a.m. as he prepares coffee and breakfast on the bottled-gas stove in the kitchen corner of the tiny house.

Isauro sees his children off to school. Sometimes he observes their classes.

Hispanic, which means that, unlike many other Spanish-Americans, Rios does not lack political representation, at least at the local level, though this hardly translates into much in the way of economic benefits. Starr County residents had in 1979 a per capita annual income of $2,668 and a median family income of $8,627. That makes Starr, according to the Census Bureau, one of the three poorest counties in a country with a national per capita income of $7,298 and a median family income of $19,917.

The Rios family's income of $8,572 puts them below even the county's median, a fact that leaves Isauro undismayed. In the morning, he gets into his faded red 1976 Nova and heads for one of the

Begoggled against dust, Rios delivers sacks of onions to a pick-up truck.

it rains, I go to school with my children. I see they have better shoes and better pencils than some of the other children. Then I think that we're doing okay."

Although he is not stuck in one of the menial, dead-end jobs that are so often the lot of poor Hispanics, Isauro has had anything but an easy life. Born in La Puerta in 1948, he was one of 14 children (including one adoptee) of a Mexican-American father and a Mexican mother. Four of his siblings have died; the 10 survivors all still live and work in the area. Four graduated from high school, to the justified pride of their family (about half the students from Spanish-speaking homes in the U.S. become high-school dropouts). Isauro finished 10th grade at the age of 15 and went to work full time.

After a stint in the military, he returned to La Puerta. By 1977 he had acquired his present job and married a young Mexican woman six years his junior, whom he had first met at a dance in Starr County's one big town, Rio Grande City (population 8,930).

county's big corporate-owned truck farms, where he drives a tractor 10 hours a day, seven days a week, for $3.45 an hour—10 cents above the legal minimum wage. During a recent year, bad weather kept him idle about a third of the time, yet he considered himself lucky to have a steady job, in a county where unemployment was more than three times the national average, and felt hopeful that he could eventually ascend to a less weather-sensitive job offering more hours of work and hence more money.

"There are people who work where I do that make $10,000 a year," he says. "Maybe soon I will make that much." Even if he does not, however, nothing will deter his drive towards a better life for himself and his family.

"Sometimes we are poor—when it rains, and I haven't been able to work," he says. "But I'm better off than most people. Sometimes when

Isauro checks a wall of the new home as Maria Jesús and two daughters look on.

Juan Carlos concentrates on a project of his own while behind him his father adds another block to the future *casa Rios*.

On a plot of land bought from a neighbour, he and his wife, Maria Jesús, built themselves a one-room home, 1.8 by 3.6 metres, floored with plywood and roofed with corrugated iron sheeting.

Four years later, Isauro and Maria Jesús began building a larger, breeze-block house on the slope behind their present one. With occasional help from a neighbour who has completed a similar house, they have been working at it for two years, and since they have four growing children (Wencelada, 7; Juan Carlos, 6; Maria Oneida, 5; and baby Erica, 18 months), the need for more living space has become increasingly pressing.

With its three bedrooms, kitchen and indoor bathroom (replacing the present outside toilet), the house will cost the Rios family about $4,000. Work proceeds intermittently, whenever there is money for building materials to spare from either Isauro's wages or what Maria Jesús earns from harvesting onions in the spring. "Maybe this year we'll finish it," says Isauro optimistically.

If not this year, then next, but finished it will be. Isauro Rios is not easily diverted from his goals. He could choose to earn more money as a migrant farm worker, as most of his neighbours do, but at the cost of dragging his family with him from job to job, depriving the children of schooling. "I want them to finish school," he says. "My son sometimes wants to go with me and ride on my tractor. But I always say I'm not taking him down there. I don't want him to learn to drive a tractor. I want him to go to college."

145

6

and his boss advised him: start your own business. "All you'll ever get working for me is $400 or $500 a week," he was told.

So Kwon went into the grocery trade. Hours before dawn, Kwon is at the Hunts Point market—the city's main distribution centre, in the South Bronx—selecting lettuce, onions, tomatoes, beans, oranges, apricots, persimmons and haggling over prices; then he loads the heavy crates into his lorry. Back at his store, helped by his wife and brother, he scrubs each fruit and vegetable in cold water, polishes it dry, and stacks it into one of the tempting pyramids that are a trademark of Korean grocers. At 8 a.m. he is open for business. For the next 12 hours the day stretches into a numbing routine of serving, restocking bins, tending the register. Then home to dinner, paperwork, a good-night kiss for his children and four or five hours of sleep before the next day starts.

Kwon's business is small; he earns a bit more than he did as a foreman, but he never expects to get rich. "I am the first generation," he proclaims. "I am not working for myself. I am working for the second generation."

It is a time-honoured sentiment in the United States. Nearly 200 years ago, John Adams, the nation's second President, wrote that he studied politics so that his sons might be free to engage in commerce and agriculture, and that their sons might devote their energies to "painting, poetry, music, architecture". Indeed, he spawned an illustrious parade of statesmen, businessmen, historians, writers and art collectors. Kwon's children and grandchildren may well grow up to become doctors, or lawyers, or scientists, or poets and artists. If so, they will have

A child waits patiently while her mother examines the produce in a Chicago greengrocer's, one of hundreds of Korean-owned enterprises that are springing up around the country.

followed a well-trodden path to the realization of American Dreams.

That path is usually education. John Adams, a farmer's son, graduated from Harvard College in 1755. He applied his education to advance himself and to prepare the way for his descendants. People in the U.S. have been following his example ever since, aided by a system that is meant to be as egalitarian as possible. It differs from education in other countries in significant respects, providing never-ending opportunities to learn about an astonishing variety of subjects.

In most of the industrialized world, every child is expected to get about 10 years of basic schooling; but at the age of 18 or so, a strict selection process—the *baccalauréat* in France, the *Abitur* in West Germany, and the *Nyugaku shiken* in Japan—determines who goes on. Those who are not in the élite group chosen for further schooling are essentially barred from the higher levels of their societies. No such cutoff exists in the United States. Education may be no less crucial to success there than elsewhere, but it can be acquired at any age, in innumerable ways.

Horace Mann, the 19th-century educationist considered the father of

the American public school system, called education "the great equalizer of the condition of men—the balance wheel of the social machinery." In the U.S. it has been just that. For the poor immigrants who poured into the country by the millions during the 19th century and the first part of the 20th, the basic public schools must have seemed heaven-sent. Here was a chance for their offspring to learn not only English, but American ways. By the early 20th century, all American children were expected to complete 12 years of schooling; the high-school diploma thus earned was an essential passport to a good job. The number of years spent in school continued to increase, as university training, then graduate study, became the norm.

Today, 86 per cent of the population completes the 12 years of the public school programme, and 12.5 million are enrolled in colleges and universities. Most people pursuing higher education—proportionately more than in any other nation—do so in what is now considered the normal manner, that is, as full-time students in successive years of their youth. But this is not the only route to education.

As many as 42 per cent of that 12.5 million attend class part time, many of them at night and many in community colleges like the one that helped Michael Blumenthal get started. Some four million study at home with correspondence courses. Opportunities for education are always available, everywhere and at every stage of life. Almost 12 per cent of the people enrolled in courses for college credit are 35 or older. At commencement time all over the country, newspapers publish pictures of middle-aged mothers in cap and gown, receiving university diplomas at

Grabbing a pizza between calls, traders at a major Wall Street investment banking firm spare no time for lunch. Such non-stop working days contribute to the high incidence of heart attacks, ulcers and other stress-related ailments in the United States.

147

the same time as their children get their own degrees.

Much of American education is job-oriented, intended to pave the way towards material success. Some 60 per cent of the courses studied by adults are taken to get a job or advance in a job. Even such renowned centres of scholarship as the University of California and the University of Wisconsin are "land-grant" institutions, founded with government support as colleges stressing the practical arts of agriculture and engineering. But along with such training goes the study of ideals: reliance on individual freedom and responsibility, a need to better the world, a willingness—almost a compulsion—to challenge accepted doctrine. The do-gooders, the dropouts and the rebels as well as the successful entrepreneurs learnt their lessons in school. And they, too, fulfil their dreams.

One who did is Kathleen Kinkade. At the age of 34, taking a night course in philosophy at Citrus Junior College in the Los Angeles area, she read *Walden Two* by the renowned behavioural psychologist B. F. Skinner. It described a utopian community, in which people's responses are reinforced or discouraged by a system of rewards and punishments. This scheme struck Kinkade as "a brilliant flash of light". She read other utopian tracts, and the accounts of various 19th-century utopian communities such as Oneida Community in New York. And she resolved to start her own commune.

In 1967, Kinkade, with seven other charter members, raised money for a down payment on a Virginian farmhouse and 40 hectares of tobacco fields. Eager but untutored in the ways of farm life, they tried to harvest the tobacco—with dismal results. Early efforts with

cows, then poultry, were equally ineffective; it was cheaper to buy milk and eggs at the supermarket. Yet somehow the commune survived, its 80 members growing most of their own food and bringing in needed cash by weaving hammocks for sale.

"We are still after the big dream," Kinkade says, "a better world, here and now, for as many people as we can manage to support. More, a new kind of human to live in that world: happy, productive, open-minded people who understand that in the long run, human good is a cooperative and not a competitive thing."

Dreams like hers almost always fall short. The history of American communes has few long-term successes. Among the better-known utopian communities, Brook Farm lasted about five years, Oneida 30, and New Harmony 15. So it is with the other dreams,

whether of a better society, a different lifestyle or material success. For all those who achieve their goals, there are many who fail. People who, in other cultures, might be content with their lot are lured—even impelled—to pursue what author William James called "the bitch goddess success".

The strains of striving are great, and the social cost is high. If current rates continue, one in every two recent marriages in the U.S. will end in divorce. Drug addiction is a massive problem—four to five million Americans use cocaine regularly. Drug counsellors estimate that between half a million and two million are profoundly dependent on heroin or cocaine. Stress among business executives is so severe that 20 per cent of the 500 largest corporations have set up programmes to help employees cope.

There can be no more embittering experience, particularly for an underprivileged member of society, than to come within reach of the American Dream and be ill-prepared to seize it. This happened to Dwight Johnson, a hero of the Vietnam War.

Johnson grew up in Detroit in a run-down black neighbourhood. He never knew his natural father. A bright, skinny boy, whom his mother called Skip, he was often chased home by bullies. "Mama, what do I do if they catch me?" he asked. "Don't you fight, honey," she told Skip, "and don't let them catch you." He became an altar boy and an Explorer Scout and, when old enough, a soldier.

It was in Vietnam that his life changed. Assigned to an armoured unit, Johnson developed a strong bond with the other men in his tank crew, and he resented a sudden transfer to another tank. The day after his trans-

Moments after receiving their degrees, two gleeful college graduates cavort barefoot in a fountain in New York City. In the early 1980s, more than a third of American 18 to 20 year olds were in college.

fer, he was riding down the road with his new crew when they were ambushed. Two of the platoon's four tanks were hit by rockets. When Johnson saw that one of them was his old tank, he leapt from the turret, ran through the enemy fire to the burning tank and threw open the hatch. He dragged out one badly burnt crewman—but before he could help his other friends, the tank blew up.

Enraged, Johnson went after the enemy. He killed 20 of them.

"When it was over," a friend said, "it took three men and three shots of morphine to hold Dwight down."

For his "uncommon valour", Johnson was awarded the Congressional Medal of Honour, the nation's highest award, in a White House ceremony. And then his troubles began.

Johnson was Michigan's only living Medal of Honour winner—and the state, the army and private industry made much of it. He was fêted and honoured and offered a variety of well-paid jobs. He was given a testimonial dinner attended by 1,500 guests, including General William C. Westmoreland, former commander of U.S. forces in Vietnam. He was lent an expensive car, granted credit in shops, and urged to study to become a lawyer; his tuition would be paid by the black business community.

Johnson had a great opportunity in his hands, but unfortunately he was unable to use it. "What does he do when he's introduced to Bunkie Knudsen, the President of Ford?" asked a lawyer friend. "Does he come across strong and dynamic because he knows there is a $75,000-a-year job waiting for him if he makes a good impression? And what happens to him when he just stands there and fumbles and doesn't know if he should shake hands or just nod his head? Johnson was forced to

play a role he was never trained for and never anticipated."

The pressure took its toll, physically and emotionally. He told a psychiatrist treating him that the public affairs he had attended had made him feel inadequate. People he met would shake his hand and slap him on the back and tell him to get in touch about a job—yet when he called, he would have to remind them who he was. The car lent to him was taken away, and he was unable to pay for repairs on a car he purchased for himself, nor could he pay the interest payments on the house he had bought. When his wife had to go to the hospital, he lacked even the $25 deposit that was required.

A few days later Dwight Johnson was shot and killed trying to hold up a store. Said his mother, "Sometimes I wonder if Skip tired of his life and needed someone to pull the trigger."

That this tragedy struck an impoverished black is understandable. Many of them find the American Dreams beyond their reach. A black who did succeed, the New York businessman Lloyd Williams, said that half the men with whom he grew up were dead or addicted, or had vanished. William Beckham Jr., a corporation vice president and a former Assistant Secretary of Transportation, said that in spite of his achievements, he was never able to forget that he was black; white people would not let him. Yet it was also Beckham who said that black Americans are, after all, Americans who "buy the American idea".

Roy Levy Williams, a black leader in Detroit, agrees. "Blacks bought into the American Dream even more than whites," he said. "They believe if you work for it in America, you'll get it, or your kids will get it."

A DIVERSITY OF RELIGIONS

Drawn by the promise of a better life, immigrants to the United States have brought with them not only their hopes but their religions. In a country founded on religious freedom, Americans in turn have created and exported new Christian denominations of their own: Christian Science, Jehovah's Witnesses and the Church of Jesus Christ of Latter-day Saints (the Mormon Church). Christianity remains the dominant religion in this pluralistic society—Roman Catholics number more than 51 million, Protestants more than 73 million. But there are also nearly six million Jews—40 per cent of the world's Jewish population—and three million Muslims.

Nowhere is the country's religious diversity more readily apparent than in New York City, where there are 1,256 synagogues, 1,766 Protestant, 437 Roman Catholic and 66 Orthodox churches, among others. In one 5-kilometre square area of Manhattan, as the pictures on these and the following pages reveal, New Yorkers can worship in at least eight different ways.

Friends and family look on as a baby undergoes a Mormon ceremony called "the blessing of the child". Organized in 1830, the Church of Jesus Christ of Latter-day Saints had 2.8 million members in 1980.

While two women wait their turn, a man is baptized by total immersion at a Southern Baptist Church. With 14 million members, the Southern Baptist Convention is the largest Protestant denomination in the U.S.

Catholics attend Mass in a church copied after Les Invalides in Paris; in 1979 there were nearly 18,700 Roman Catholic parishes in the country.

Costumed youths perform a drum ceremony called *taiko* in a Buddhist temple hall; there are 150,000 Buddhists in the United States.

One of America's 550 Greek Orthodox churches celebrates Greek Independence Day.

Lutheran ministers serve Holy Communion; U.S. Lutherans number about 8,596,000.

A wedding ceremony is performed by a minister of the Korean United Church, a Presbyterian denomination. Presbyterians in the United States number four million.

A 13-year old boy is called up to the reading of the Torah during his bar mitzvah, a Jewish ritual denoting that he has attained religious maturity. Of the country's six million Jews, two million live in New York City.

ACKNOWLEDGEMENTS

The index for this book was prepared by Barbara L. Klein. For their help in the preparation of this volume, the editors wish to thank: Kate Alfriend, U.S. Dept. of Agriculture, Washington, D.C.; California State Dept. of Agriculture, Sacramento; G. William Domhoff, Adlai E. Stevenson College, University of California, Santa Cruz; Jamie Gipe, Waco, Texas; Joe Goodwin, Washington, D.C.; Vance Grant, Dept. of Education, Washington, D.C.; Kathy Kajari, Chicago Police Dept.; Steve Lawson, Dept. of History, University of South Florida, Tampa; Chuck E. Little, American Land Forum, Bethesda, Md.; Carol Lutyk, National Geographic Society, Washington, D.C.; Major Alex L. Mondragon, Infantry, United States Military Academy, West Point, N.Y.; Kay Mussell, The American University, Washington, D.C.; Dave Nicholl, President, Winterset Chamber of Commerce, Winterset, Iowa; Norman Ornstein, American Enterprise Institute, Washington, D.C.; Wayne D. Rasmussen, U.S. Dept. of Agriculture, Washington, D.C.; John Rorke, Millbrook School, Millbrook, N.Y.

PICTURE CREDITS

Credits from left to right are separated by semicolons, from top to bottom by dashes.

Cover: Harald Sund, Seattle. Front and back endpapers: Maps by Lloyd K. Townsend. Back endpaper: Map digitized by Creative Data, London.

1, 2: © Flag Research Center, Winchester, Massachusetts. 6, 7: John T. Hill, courtesy City Investing Company, New York. 8, 9: Shelly Katz from Black Star, New York. Chart digitized by Creative Data, London. 10–13: Nathan Benn from Woodfin Camp, Washington, D.C. Charts digitized by Creative Data, London. 14, 15: George Herben from Woodfin Camp & Associates, New York. Chart digitized by Creative Data, London. 17: Brown Brothers, Sterling, Pennsylvania. 18, 19: Rick Morley from West Stock, Seattle, Washington. 20: © David Muench 1983, Santa Barbara, California. 22, 23: Nathan Benn from Woodfin Camp, Washington, D.C. 24: Barry Kaplan from The Stock Market, New York. 25: Kenneth Garrett from Woodfin Camp, Washington, D.C. 26, 27: Robert Frerck, Odyssey Productions, Chicago. 29–35: Winnie Denker, New York. 37: Craig Aurness from West Light, Los Angeles. 38: Derosnay from Gamma-Liaison, New York. 39: Tim Thompson, Bainbridge Island, Washington. 40–53: Winnie Denker, New York. 54, 55: Jonathan Wallen, New York. 57: Courtesy of The Pennsylvania Academy of the Fine Arts, Philadelphia. 58: Library of Congress, Washington; except lower left, *Penn's Treaty With The Indians*, Edward Hicks, National Gallery of Art, Washington, D.C., gift of Edgar William and Bernice Chrysler Garbisch 1980. 59: Worcester Art Museum, Worcester, Massachusetts; *Prisoners From The Front*, Winslow Homer, courtesy the Metropolitan Museum of Art, New York, gift of Mrs. Frank B. Porter 1922—Alexander Gardner, courtesy Dorothy Meserve Kunhardt Trust, Chappaqua, New York. 60: Library of Congress; Wide World Photos, New York; John Olson for *Life*— Courtesy Time Inc. 62: Courtesy of the U.S. Naval Academy Museum, Annapolis, Maryland. 63: Courtesy the William Turner Collection, Clinton, Maryland. 64, 65: Smithsonian Institution National Anthropological Archives, Bureau of American Ethnology Collection, Washington, D.C. 66: Library of Congress, Washington. 68, 69: Winnie Denker, New York. 70, 71: Robert Frerck, Odyssey Productions, Chicago. 73: Robert Frerck, Chicago. 74, 76: Chuck O'Rear from West Light, Los Angeles. 77: Eric Kroll, New York. 78, 79: William Garnett, Napa, California. 80: Robert Frerck, Odyssey Productions, Chicago. 82: Maxwell Mackenzie, Washington, D.C. 84–91: Winnie Denker, New York. 92: From *Jukebox: The Golden Age*, Lancaster Miller & Schnobrich Publishers, Berkeley, California, photograph by Kazuhiro Tsuruta. 94: Henry Groskinsky for *Life*. 95: *Untitled*, Alexander Calder, National Gallery of Art, Washington, D.C., gift of the Collectors Committee 1977. 96: Frank Driggs Collection, New York. 99: Winnie Denker, New York, except upper right: Michael O'Brien from Archive, New York. 101: © 1939 Walt Disney Productions, Burbank, California. 102: Courtesy Time Inc. 103: Acme/Wide World, New York. 104: Orlando/Gamma-Liaison, New York. 106–111: Ethan Hoffman from Archive, New York. 112, 113: Nathan Benn, Washington, D.C. 114, 115: Michael O'Brien from Archive, New York. 116: Nathan Benn from Woodfin Camp, Washington, D.C. 117: Erich Hartmann from Magnum, New York. 120: The Bancroft Library, University of California, Berkeley. 123: Bill Fitzpatrick from The White House, Washington, D.C. 124: Wide World Photos, New York. 126–135: Winnie Denker, New York. 136, 137: Michael O'Brien © 1983 National Geographic Society, Washington, D.C. 138: Robert Frerck, Odyssey Productions, Chicago. 139: Jose Anzel from Contact Stock Images. 141–145: Max Aguilera Hellweg, New York. 146: Robert Frerck, Odyssey Productions, Chicago. 147: Katherine Lambert from Black Star, New York. 148: Joan Lifton from Archive, New York. 149: Chuck Fishman, New York. 150–155: Winnie Denker, New York.

BIBLIOGRAPHY

BOOKS

Babcock, C. Merton, *The American Frontier: A Social Literary Record*. Holt, Rinehart and Winston, 1965.

Balliett, Whitney, *Such Sweet Thunder: Forty-Nine Pieces on Jazz*. Bobbs-Merrill, 1966.

Battison, Edwin, A., and Patricia Kane, *The American Clock 1725–1865*. New York Graphic Society, 1973.

Bayer, William, *The Great Movies*. Grossett & Dunlap, 1973.

Billington, Ray A., Samuel H. Brockunier and Bert J. Lowenburg, eds., *The Making of American Democracy: Readings and Documents*. Vols. I and II, Rinehart, 1950.

Birdsall, Stephen S., and John W. Florin, *Regional Landscapes of the United States and Canada*. Wiley, 1981.

Boorstin, Daniel J., Brooks Mather Kelley and Ruth Frankel Boorstin, *A History of the United States*. Ginn, 1981.

Buerkle, Jack V., and Danny Barker, *Bourbon Street Black: The New Orleans Black Jazzman*. Oxford University Press, 1973.

Busnar, Gene, *It's Rock 'n' Roll*. Julian Messner, 1979.

Chamberlain, John, *The Enterprising Americans: A Business History of the United States*. Harper & Row, 1963.

Chilton, John, *Who's Who of Jazz*. Chilton, 1972.

Clawson, Marion, *America's Land and Its Uses*. Johns Hopkins, 1972.

Congressional Quarterly:
Editorial Research Reports on America in the 1980s. Congressional Quarterly, 1979.
Editorial Research Reports on American Regionalism. Congressional Quarterly, 1980.
Editorial Research Reports on The Changing American Family. Congressional Quarterly, 1979.
Revolution in Civil Rights. Congressional Quarterly. 1968.

Current, Richard, and John A. Garraty, eds., *Words that Made American History*. Vols. I and II. Little, Brown, 1965.

Dance, Stanley, *The World of Duke Ellington*. Charles Scribner's Sons, 1970.

Davidson, Roger H., and Walter Z. Oleszek, *Congress and Its Members*. Congressional Quarterly, 1981.

Delaunay, Charles, *New Hot Discography: The Standard Directory of Recorded Jazz*. Criterion, 1948.

Detholff, Henry, *Americans and Free Enterprise*. Prentice-Hall, 1979.

Domhoff, G. William, *The Bohemian Grove and Other Retreats*. Harper & Row, 1974.

Dye, Thomas R., *Who's Running America?* Prentice-Hall, 1979.

The Editors of American Heritage Magazine, *American Heritage New Pictorial Encyclopedic Guide to the United States.* Dell, 1965.

Ellington, Edward Kennedy, *Music is My Mistress.* Da Capo, 1976.

Everson, William K., *American Silent Film.* Oxford University Press, 1978.

Fawcett, Edmund, and Tony Thomas, *The American Condition.* Harper & Row, 1982.

Feather, Leonard, *The New Edition of The Encyclopedia of Jazz.* Bonanza, 1960.

Fornatale, Peter, and Joshua E. Mills, *Radio in the Television Age.* Overlook, 1980.

Gabriel, Ralph H., *American Values, Continuity and Change.* Greenwood, 1974.

Garraty, John A., *The American Nation.* American Heritage, 1966.

Garreau, Joel, *The Nine Nations of North America.* Avon, 1981.

Garrow, David J., *Protest at Selma.* Yale University Press, 1978.

Gastil, Raymond D., *Cultural Regions of the United States.* University of Washington Press, 1975.

Gilbert, Annie, *All My Afternoons.* A & W Publishers, 1979.

Graber, Doris A., *Mass Media and American Politics.* Congressional Quarterly. 1980.

Green, Stanley, *The World of Musical Comedy.* A. S. Barnes, 1980.

Harris, H. G., *19th Century American Clocks.* Emerson, 1981.

Head, Sidney W., *Broadcasting in America.* Houghton Mifflin, 1972.

Hofstadter, Richard, *The American Political Tradition.* Vintage/Random House, 1974.

Jablonski, Edward, and Lawrence D. Stewart, *The Gershwin Years.* Doubleday, 1973.

Johnson, E.A.J., and Herman E. Krooss, *The American Economy: Its Origins, Development and Transformation.* Prentice-Hall, 1960.

Jones, Maldwyn Allen, *American Immigration.* University of Chicago Press, 1960.

Kardish, Laurence, *Reel Plastic Magic: A History of Films and Filmmaking in America.* Little, Brown, 1972.

Keynes, Edward, and David Adamany, eds., *The Borzoi Reader in American Politics.* Knopf, 1971.

Kinkade, Kathleen, *A Walden Two Experiment.* Morrow, 1974.

Kramer, Mark, *Making Meat, Milk and Money from the American Soil.* Little, Brown, 1980.

Lahue, Kalton C., *World of Laughter: The Motion Picture Comedy Short, 1919–1930.* University of Oklahoma Press, 1966.

Lahue, Kalton C., and Terry Brewer, *Kops and Custards: The Legend of Keystone Films.* University of Oklahoma Press, 1968.

Least Heat Moon, William, *Blue Highways.* Little, Brown, 1982.

Lipson, Harry A., and John R. Darling, *Marketing Fundamentals: Text and Cases.* Wiley, 1974.

Livesay, Harold C., *American Made: Men Who Shaped the American Economy.* Little, Brown, 1979.

Moore, N. Hudson, *The Old Clock Book.* Tudor, 1936.

Morison, Samuel Eliot, *The Oxford History of the American People.* Vols. I, II and III. New American Library, 1972.

Morrison, Joan, and Charlotte Fox Zabusky, *American Mosaic.* Dutton, 1980.

Nash, Roderick, "American Space", *The American Land.* Smithsonian Exposition Book, 1979.

Newcomb, Horace, *Television: The Critical View.* Oxford University Press, 1976.

Nye, Russel, *The Unembarrassed Muse: The Popular Arts in America.* Dial, 1970.

O'Neill, Thomas, *Back Roads America.* National Geographic Society, 1980.

Ornstein, Norman J., and Shirley Elder, *Interest Groups, Lobbying and Policymaking.* Congressional Quarterly, 1978.

Palmer, Tony, *All You Need Is Love: The Story of Popular Music.* Penguin, 1977.

Parkinson, Michael, and Clyde Jeavons, *A Pictorial History of Westerns.* Hamlyn, 1973.

Poulson, Barry W., *Economic History of the United States.* Macmillan, 1981.

Quint, Howard H., Milton Canton and Dean Albertson, eds., *Main Problems in American History.* Vols I and II. Dorsey, 1978.

Reeves, Richard, *American Journey.* Simon and Schuster, 1982.

Reid, T. R., *Congressional Odyssey.* W. H. Freeman, 1980.

Roberts, Gene, and David R. Jones, eds., *Assignment America.* Quadrangle/The New York Times, 1974.

Robertson, James Oliver, *American Myth, American Reality.* Hill & Wang, 1980.

Rotkin, Charles, *The U.S.A.: An Aerial Close-up.* Crown. 1968.

Schuller, Gunther, *Early Jazz: Its Roots and Musical Development.* Oxford University Press, 1968.

Schwartz, Charles, *Gershwin: His Life and Music.* Bobbs-Merrill, 1973.

Sheehy, Gail, *Pathfinders.* Morrow, 1981.

Shenton, James P., *History of the United States from 1865 to the Present.* Doubleday, 1964.

Slappey, Sterling G., *Pioneers of American Business.* Grosset & Dunlap, 1973.

Terkel, Studs, *American Dreams, Lost and Found.* Pantheon, 1980.

Wakefield, Dan, *All Her Children.* Doubleday, 1976.

Watson, Richard A., *Promise and Performance of American Democracy.* Wiley, 1981.

Wilk, Max, *The Golden Age of Television: Notes from the Survivors.* Delacorte, 1976.

Zelinsky, Wilbur, *The Cultural Geography of the United States.* Prentice-Hall. 1973.

PERIODICALS

Agee, James, "Comedy's Greatest Era." *Life,* September 5, 1949.

"American Survey: New York City." *The Economist,* April 2, 1983.

Andersen, Kurt, "The New Ellis Island." *Time,* June 13, 1983.

Batie, Sandra S., and Robert G. Healy, "The Future of American Agriculture." *Scientific American,* February 1983.

Blow, Steve, "Where Dignity Triumphs: Life in Starr County, Texas." *Parade,* May 22, 1983.

Bradshaw, Ted K., "California: Trying Out the Future." *Wilson Quarterly,* Summer 1980.

Cocks, Jay, "American Women: The Climb to Equality." *Time,* July 12, 1982.

"Economic Report of the President." GPO, February 1983.

The Editors of *Wilson Quarterly:*

"The Changing Family." *Wilson Quarterly,* Winter, 1977.

"The Public Schools." *Wilson Quarterly,* Autumn, 1979.

Hedberg, Augustin, "How to Change Your Life." *Money,* May 1982.

Henry, William A., III, "Against a Confusion of Tongues." *Time,* June 13, 1983.

"It's Your Turn in the Sun." *Time,* October 16, 1978.

Johnston, Moira, "Silicon Valley—Cradle of the Chip." *National Geographic,* October 1982.

Morgan, Thomas B., "The Latinization of America." *Esquire,* May 1983.

Morganthau, Tom, "America's Small Town Boom." *Newsweek,* July 6, 1981.

"A Portrait of America: Who We Are and How We Are Changing." *Newsweek,* January 17, 1983.

Rawls, James J., "California: Visions and Revisions." *Wilson Quarterly,* Summer 1980.

Thurber, James, "Soapland." *The New Yorker,* May 15, May 29, June 12, July 24, 1948.

Trippett, Frank, "Small Town, U.S.A.: Growing and Groaning." *Time,* September 1, 1980.

U.S. Department of Agriculture, *1983 Fact Book of U.S. Agriculture.* GPO, 1982.

U.S. News & World Report, *The ABC of How Your Government Works.* May 9, 1977.

White, Peter T., "This Land of Ours—How Are We Using It?" *National Geographic,* July 1976.

Woodbridge, Sally B., "The California House." *Wilson Quarterly,* Summer 1980.

INDEX

Page numbers in italics refer to illustrations or illustrated text.

A

Abolitionists, 62
Adams, Brock, quoted, 121
Adams, John, 61, 146
Advertising, 83
Age, increasing, in U.S., *chart* 12
Agee, James, quoted, 100
Agribusiness, 80–81
Agriculture, 8, 76–81; corporate farms, 80, 81; family farms, 80–81, *84–91*; land, *25, 77–79*
Alabama, black-vote issue in, 123–125
Alaska, *14–15,* 36–37, *39,* 58, 59, 60
Alda, Alan, *104*
Alien and Sedition Acts, 61
American Revolution, 56, *58,* 59
Amish sect, Indiana, *46, 47*
Andrews, Robert Douglas Hardy, 104
Anti-trust actions, 65
Armstrong, Louis, 94, 95
Arnaz, Desi, 105
Arts and culture, 93–105; artefacts, *92, 94, 95, 99;* artists, 93; composers, 93, 94, 95–98; films, 93, 98, 100–103, *101–103;* jazz, 93, 94–97; musicals, 97–98; musicians, 94–97, *96, 106–113;* radio, 93–94, 103–105; television, 93–94, 103, *104,* 105; writers, 93
Ashley, Ricanthony R., *68*
Assembly line, *74–75*
Astaire, Fred, *102*
Atkins, Beth, and family, 126, *127–135*

B

Ball, Lucille, 105
Balliett, Whitney, quoted, 96
Baltimore, 24
Baptists and baptism, *150–151*
Bar mitzvah, *154–155*
Barge lines, legislation affecting, 119–123
Basie, Count, 97
Bass, Angela, *34*
Beasley, Charles, and son, *109*
Bechet, Sidney, 95–96
Beckham, William Jr., 149
Berlin, Irving, 97, 98
Bill of Rights, 57, 59
Bills, legislative: civil rights, 60, 67; voting rights, 67, 124–125; waterways, 120–123
Birth of a Nation (film), 98
Black, William, 140
Blacks: and American Dream, 139–140, 148–149; civil rights movement (1960s), 67, 123–125, *124;* musicians, 94–97, *96, 106–113;* slavery, 59, 60, 62–63; in the South, 28, 122–125
Blatt, Solomon, *114–115*
Blumenthal, W. Michael, 137–139

Board of Trade, Chicago, *73*
Boggs, Hale, quoted, 125
Bohemian Grove, California, *120*
Boston, 23–24; Massacre, 58; Tea Party, *58*
Bridges: covered, Iowa, *46;* George Washington, *43;* at Great Falls, *44–45;* Oakland Bay, *52–53*
British imperialism, 56
Bryant, Arthur, 26
Buddhists, *152–153*
Burke Hollow, town meeting, *16*

C

Calder, Alexander, mobile by, *95*
Calhoun, John C., 61, 63, 67
California, 20, 36, 38–41, *52–53;* agriculture, *78–79,* 81; Bohemian Grove, *120;* computer promotion, *76;* hot tub, *40–41;* Hollywood, 38, 93, 94, 100, 101, 103; Imperial Valley, 21; Los Angeles, *3, 9,* 41; Sacramento Valley, *78–79;* San Francisco, 38, *52–53;* San Joaquin Valley, 81; sequoias, *20;* solar electrical generating plant, *70–71*
Camera (Polaroid), 75
Carefree (film), *102*
Carnegie, Andrew, 72, 74
Cars, 42–53; Los Angeles, 41; Presley's, *99;* production, *74–75*
Carter, Jimmy, 26, 121, 122
Cartoons, animated, *101*
Cascade Range, *18–19*
Catholics, *152–153*
Chaplin, Charles, 100
Charter of Privileges, *58*
Cheerleaders, *34–35*
Cherokee Outlet, 21
Chicago, *26–27;* airport, 80; barman, *45;* Board of Trade, *73;* city council, 117; greengrocer, *146;* police officers, *126–135;* St. Patrick's Day in, *138*
Christianity, *150–154*
City Lights (film), 100
Civil rights movements, 67, 123–125, *124*
Civil War, *59,* 63–64
Clark, Jim, 124
Clay, Henry, quoted, 118
Clift, Montgomery, *103*
Clocks, history of mass production, 71–72
Cody, Buffalo Bill, 47
College education, 24, 146, 148
Colonial history, 55–56, *58*
Columbia River, 38
Commodities exchange, *73*
Communes, utopian, 139, 148
Computer-based technology, 75–76
Congress, 118, 119; voting rights bill, 125; waterways bill, 119–123
Constitution, 19, 55, 56–57, 63, 66, 118; Amendments, 19, 57, 59, 60, 63, 66
Constitution (warship), *62*

Continental Congress, 56
Coolidge, Calvin, 23
Corporate farms, 80, 81
Culture. *See* Arts and culture

D

Dallas, 35
Dallas (TV programme), 105
Declaration of Independence, 55, 63
Democratic Party in Chicago, 117
Depression (1930s), 66; migration during, *66*
Dick, Minnie, *49*
Didion, Joan, quoted, 40, 41
Dieterich, Ben, and family, *84–91*
Dirksen, Everett, quoted, 119
Disney, Walter Elias, 101
Dixie, 28, 35
Domenici, Pete V., proposal by, 119–123
Durant, William C., 75
Dutcher, Dino D., *68*
Dye, Thomas R., 117, 119

E

Eagle Gate, Salt Lake City, *49*
Eames, Charles, chair designed by, *94*
Earthquakes, 41
Economy: agriculture, 76–77, *77–79,* 79–81, *84–91;* fiscal and monetary policies, 76; government and, 76, 77, 79; occupations, *chart* 8; prosperity, 72, 140; service industries, *8–9,* 72, 81, 83; traders, *73, 147. See also* Industry
Education, 24, 146, 148
Electronics industry, 75–76
Ellington, Edward Kennedy (Duke), 94–95, *96–97*
Ellis Island, immigrants on, *7, 17*
Energy production, *chart* 15
Equal rights movements, 67, 123–125, *124*
Ethnic groups, 21; in ancestry, 68–69; Haitians, *77;* Hawaii, 37; Hispanics, 140, *141–145;* Koreans, 140, 146; Los Angeles, 41; New York City, 24, 140, 146. *See also* Blacks

F

Fast-food business, 83
Feeney, J. D., 121
Films, 93, 98; animated, *101;* comedy, 98, 100–101; musical, *102;* Western, 101–*103*
Florida: agriculture, *77;* centenarians, *12–13*
Fons, Marianne, *33*
Ford, Henry, 74–75
French Market Jazz Band, *108–109*
Frontier era, 16
Frost, Robert, quoted, 20

G

Garrison, William Lloyd, 62
General Motors (GM), 75
George III, King (Great Britain), 56

Georgetown Park (shopping centre), *82*
Gershwin, George and Ira, 97
Government, 115–125; Chicago, 117; colonial, 55, 56; and economy, 76–77, 79; elitist vs. pluralist system, 116–117, 119, 120; groups affecting, 115–116; lawmaking process, 119–123, 124, 125; structure at federal level, *chart* 118; town meetings, 24, *116. See also* History
Great Falls, Paterson, *44–45*
Great Lakes region, 25
Great Salt Lake region, 36
Great Train Robbery, The (film), 98
Greek Orthodox church, *153*
Greer, Sonny, quoted, 96
Griffith, David Wark, 98, 101
Grocery businesses: Korean-owned, 140, *146*; 7-Eleven, *8–9*
Gunther, John, quoted, 38–39

H

Haight-Ashbury district, San Francisco, *53*
Hamilton, Alexander, 45, 57, 61
Hammerstein, Oscar, II, 97–98
Hardy, Oliver, 100
Hart, Lorenz, 97
Harvard, 24
Hawaii, 36–37; wind-surfer, *38*
Hellman, Lillian, quoted, 21
Hesburgh, Theodore M., quoted, 20–21
Hispanics, 140, *141–145*
History, 55–67; chronology, *58–60*; civil rights movements, 67, 123–125, *124*; Civil War, *59*, 63–64; colonial, 55–56, *58*; documents, 55, 57, 59, 63, 66; expansion, 16, 61; government, formation of, 56–57; immigration, 16, *17*; Indians, *64, 65*; industry, 64–65, 71–72, 74–75; Jackson, Andrew, 61–62; Jefferson vs. Hamilton, 57, 61; Oklahoma land rush, 21; Progressives, 64–65, 66; revolution, 56, *58, 59*; Roosevelt, Franklin Delano, *60*, 66–67; Roosevelt, Theodore, 65–66; slavery, 59, 62–63; War of 1812, 61, 62
Hollywood, 38, 93, 94, 100, 101, 103
Horseback pool, *34*
Hot tub, *40–41*
House of Representatives, 122, 123, 125
Houston, 35
Hummert, Frank and Anne, 103–104
Humphrey brothers' band, *106–107*
Hutchinson, Anne, 56

I

I Love Lucy (TV programme), 105
"Illegals", Hispanic, 140
Illinois. *See* Chicago
Immigrants, 16–*17*, 41, 69; success, 140, 146
Indians, American, *49*; in history, *64, 65*
Industry, 25; car, *74–75*; corporate power, 64–65; high technology, 75–76; mass production,

71–72, *74*; new products, 75; South, 28; steel, 25–26, *45*, 72–74
Interstate 80 (highway), 42, *50–53*; sights along, *44–53*; sign, *42*
Iowa, 26, *46–47*; Winterset, 28, *29–35*

J

Jackson, Andrew, 61–62
Jackson, Jimmy Lee, 125
Jackson, Preston, *112–113*
Jazz, 94–97, *106–113*
Jefferson, Thomas, 57, *59*, 61, 123
Jews and Judaism, 150, *154–155*
Jobs, Steven, 140
Johnson, Dwight, 148–149
Johnson, James P., 94, 95
Johnson, Lyndon B., 67, 124, 125
Joplin, Scott, 94
Jukebox, *92*

K

Keaton, Buster, 100–101
Kelly, Russell, and "Kelly girls", 83
Kentucky: Pikeville, *136–137*
Kern, Jerome, 97
King, Martin Luther, Jr., 67, 123, *124*–125
Kingdome (stadium), Seattle, *18–19*
Kinkade, Kathleen, 148
Korean United Church, *154*
Koreans in U.S., 140, 146
Kroc, Ray, 83
Kwon, Young Jun, 140, 146

L

Land, Edwin, 75
Laramie, Fort, Indian treaty at, *65*
Laurel, Stan, 100
Lawmaking process, 119; voting rights bill, 124, 125; waterways bill, 119–123
Lewis, Leslie A., *68–69*
Lexington and Concord, battles of, *58*
Lincoln, Abraham, *59*, 63, 67; statue, *54–55*
Lincoln Memorial, Washington, D.C., *54–55*
Lindbergh, Charles A., *60*
Lobbyists, 119, 121
Long, Russell, 121–122
Long, Stephen, 36
Los Angeles, 39, 41
Louisiana, jazz in, *106–113*
Lutherans, *153*

M

Machine politics in Chicago, 117
Mahoning River, *45*
Maine, 21
Manhattan Island, *6–7*
Mann, Horace, quoted, 146
Marathon, New York City, *139*
Marketing, 81, 83

Maryland, 24, *25*
M*A*S*H (TV programme), *104*, 105
Mass production, 71–72; assembly line *74*
Massachusetts, 21; Boston, 23–24; history, 55–56, *58*; Institute of Technology, 24; Marblehead, *22–23*
McCloud, Jamie L., *69*
McDonald's fast-food outlets, *48*, 83
Media, 21; news, 115; TV networks, 24
Mexican-American family, *141–145*
Mickey Mouse (cartoon character), *101*
Middle Atlantic Seaboard, 24, *25, 44–45. See also* New York, N.Y.; Washington, D.C.
Mid-west, 25–26, *45–47*; Winterset, 28, *29–35. See also* Chicago
Minneapolis-St. Paul, 26
Minorities. *See* Ethnic groups
Minutemen, *58*
Monopolies, 64; actions against, 65
Monument Valley, *37*
Moore, Kevin A., *69*
Mormon Temple, Salt Lake City, *49*
Mormons, 36; ceremony, *150*
Mueller, George, *46*
Murphy, Jack, *126–127, 132*
Music, 93; musicals, 93, 97–98, 102; musicians, 94–97, *96, 106–113*; rock and roll, 98

N

National parks, 36
Nebraska: Gothenburg, *47*; Lincoln, university students in, *47*; Scout's Rest, *47*
Neufeld, Abraham, 81
Nevada, *49–51*
Nevin, John, quoted, 81
New Deal, 66–67
New England, *10–11*, 21, *22–23*, 23–24; history, 55–56, *58*; town meetings, 24, *116*
New Hampshire, 21, 24
New Jersey, *44–45*
New Orleans, jazz in, *105–113*
New York, N.Y., *6–7*, 24; banking firm, *147*; George Washington bridge, *43*; immigrants, *17*, 140, 146; marathon, *139*; religion, *150–155*
News media, 115
Nixon, Agnes, 105
Nixon, Richard, 67
North-west, *18–19*, 37–38

O

Occupations, *chart* 8; agriculture, 8, 76–77, *77–79*, 79–81, *84–91*; service industries, *8–9*, 72, 81, 83. *See also* Industry
Ohio, steel industry in, *45*
Oil: Alaska, *14–15*, 37; California, *53*
Oklahoma land rush, 21
Olds, Ransom Eli, 74
O'Neill, Thomas P. "Tip", Jr., 122, 123
Oregon, 37–38

P

Pacific states: Alaska, *14–15*, 36–37, *39*; Hawaii, 36, *38*; Pacific North-west, *18–19*, 37. *See also* California
Paine, Thomas, 56
Pal Joey (musical), 97
Paradise Valley, *50*
Parks, Gordon, quoted, 96–97
Paterson, N.J., *44–45*
Peale, Charles Wilson, painting by, *57*
Pennsylvania, 24, *44*; founding, *58*
Percy, Charles H., quoted, 121
Philanthropy, 139
Phillips, Irna, 104–105
Pipeline, trans-Alaskan, *14–15*
Plockhoy, Pieter, 139
Pluralist vs. élitist view of power structure, 116–117
Police officers, daily life of, *126–135*
Political convention, *117*
Politics, Chicago, 117
Population: age averages, *chart* 12; ancestry, *68–69*; shifts, *chart* and *map* 10
Porter, Cole, 98
Porter, Edwin, 98
Porter, Liz, *33*
Porter, Matt, *34*
Potter, David, quoted, 72
Powers, Michael, and daughter, *40–41*
Presbyterian wedding ceremony, *154*
Presley, Elvis, 98; memorabilia, *99*
Progressive movement, 64–65
Progressive Party, 66
Prohibition, 60, 66; 18th Amendment, 60, 66
Puritans, 55–56

R

Radio, 93, 103–105
Ragtime, 94
Rainier, Mount, *18–19*
Red Cloud, Chief, *64*
Red River (film), *103*
Religion, *150–155*
Reno, wedding chapel in, *50*
Revolutionary War, 56, *58*, 59
Rios, Isauro, and family, *141–145*
Roach, Hal, 100
Robots, industrial, *74*
Rock and roll, 98
Rockefeller, John D., 64
Rodgers, Richard, 97–98
Rogers, Ginger, *102*
Roman Catholics, *152–153*
Roosevelt, Franklin Delano, *60*, 66–67, 123
Roosevelt, Theodore, 65–66
Royall Street, New Orleans, *108–109*

S

St. Patrick's Day celebration, *138*

San Francisco, 39, *52–53*
Sandburg, Carl, quoted, 26
Scherm, Erna, *32*
Science and scientists, 17
Seattle, *18*
Selma, 124, 125
Senate, working of, 119–123, 125
Sennett, Mack, 98, 100
Sequoia trees, *20*
Service industries, *8–9*, 72, 81, 83
7-Eleven grocery, Dallas, *8–9*
Sheehy, Gail, 139
Sheridan, Philip, 35
Sherman Anti-Trust Act (1890), 65
Shopping centres, *82*
Show Boat (musical), 97
Siegel, Mo, 140
Sierra Nevada, *20*
Silicon Valley, 76
Skinner, B. F., 148
Slavery, 59, 62–63; 13th Amendment, 63
Sloan, Alfred P., Jr., 75
Smith, Bessie, 96
Smith, Howard, 125
Snider, John T., *69*
Soap operas, 94, 103–105
Solar electrical generating plant, *70–71*
South, 26, 28; black vote, issue of, 123–125; history, 59, 62, 63; jazz, *106–113*
Southern Baptist church, 28, *150–151*
Space programme, 17, 60
Statue of Liberty, 16, *24*
Steel industry, 25–26, *45*, 72, 74
Stein, Gertrude, quoted, 20
Steves, Jennifer, 140
Strafford, Vermont, *10–11*
Strayhorn, Billy, 97
Stroudsburg, *44*
Sumter, Fort, *59*

T

Tahoe, Lake, area, *51*, 52
Tejon Agricultural Partners (TAP), 81
Television, 93, 103, *104*, 105
Temporary-employment business, 83
Terry, Eli, 71, 72
Texas, 28, 35; Dallas, 35; families, *84–91*, *141–145*
Thoreau, Henry David, quoted, 139
Thurber, James, quoted, 103
Todd, William B., *63*
Trans-Alaskan pipeline, *14–15*
Transistors, 75
Transportation, 21, 42; buggies, Amish, *46–47*; Los Angeles, 39, 41; *see also* Cars
Treaties with Indians, 64, *65*
Truman, Harry, S., quoted, 117
Tuscarora, cemetery, *51*
Twain, Mark, quoted, 81
Two Egg, Florida, *12–13*

U

United States Steel, 121
Utah, 36; Salt Lake City, *49*
Utopian communities, 139, 148

V

Vanderbilt, Cornelius, 64
Vermont 21, 22; Craftsbury, *24*; Strafford, *10–11*; town meetings, 24, *116*
Vietnam War, *60*, 67; hero, 148–149; memorial, *149*
Voting rights, 61, 67, 123–125

W

Wallace, George C., 125
Wallace, Lisa K., *68*
War of 1812, 62
Warshow, Robert, quoted, 102
Washington, D.C., 25; memorials, *54–55*, *149*; National Gallery, *95*; shopping centre, *82*; White House, *123*
Washington, George, portrait of, *57*
Washington (state): Seattle, *18–19*, 37–38
Waterways legislation, 119–123
Wayne, John, *103*; birthplace, *31*
Weddings: ceremony, *154*; Reno chapel, *50*
West, 35–36, *37*, *48–51*, 64
West Point, cadets at, *68–69*
Western films, 101–*103*
White, George, 97
White House, *123*
Wilks, Henry G., *68*
Williams, Lloyd, 149
Williams, Roger, 55, 56
Williams, Roy Levy, quoted, 149
Willoughby, William F., *69*
Wilson, Woodrow, 66, 119
Winterset, Iowa, 28, *29–35*
Winthrop, John, 55, 56
World Trade Center, New York, N.Y., *24*
World War I poster, *60*
World War II, 60
Wozniak, Stephen, 140
Wyoming, *48*; Indian treaties, 64, 65

Z

Ziegfeld, Florenz, 97

Colour separations by Scan Studios, Ltd., Dublin, Ireland
Typesetting by Tradespools Ltd., Somerset, England

3 4 5 6 7 8 9 10 11 12 13 14 15 - IL - 90 89 88 87 86

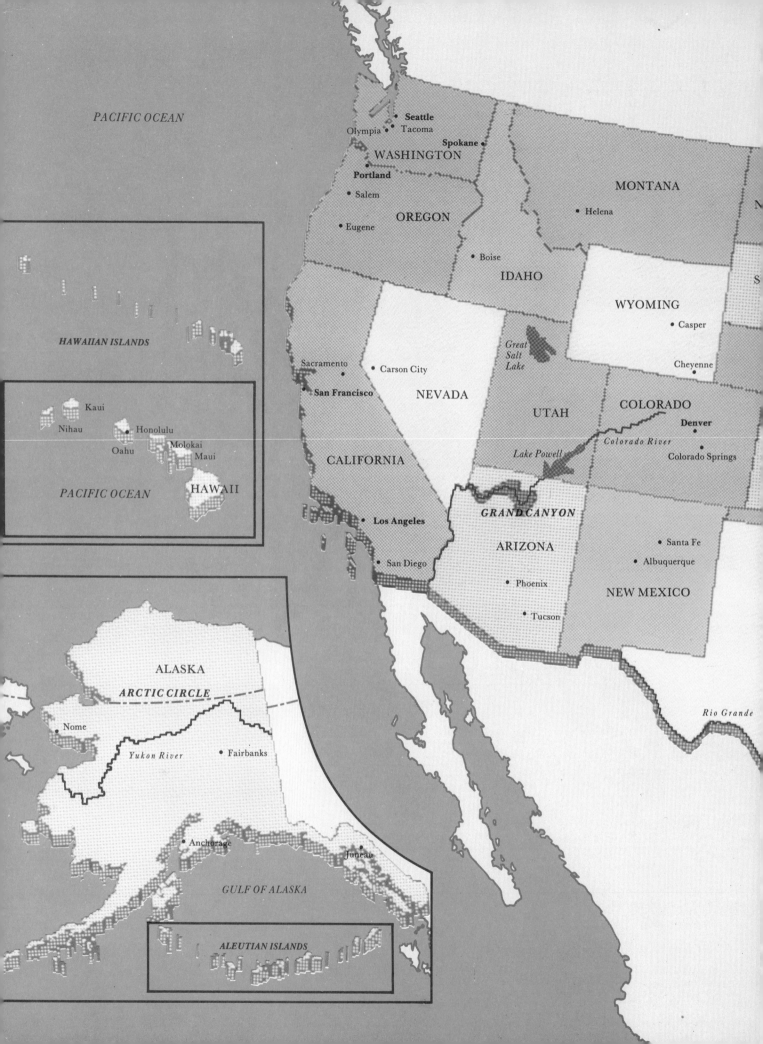

PACIFIC OCEAN

Seattle
Olympia • • Tacoma
Spokane •
WASHINGTON

Portland •

• Salem

OREGON

• Eugene

• Boise

IDAHO

MONTANA

• Helena

WYOMING

• Casper

• Cheyenne

Sacramento
• • Carson City

San Francisco •

NEVADA

Great
Salt
Lake

UTAH

COLORADO

Denver •

Colorado River

Colorado Springs

CALIFORNIA

Lake Powell

Los Angeles

• San Diego

GRAND CANYON

ARIZONA

• Phoenix

• Tucson

NEW MEXICO

• Santa Fe

• Albuquerque

HAWAIIAN ISLANDS

Kaui

Nihau

• Honolulu

Oahu

Molokai

Maui

PACIFIC OCEAN

HAWAII

ALASKA

ARCTIC CIRCLE

• Nome

Yukon River

• Fairbanks

• Anchorage

• Juneau

GULF OF ALASKA

ALEUTIAN ISLANDS

Rio Grande